# KEEPER OF STYLE

# KEEPER OF STYLE

## JOHN MURRAY: THE KING OF LORD'S

CHRISTOPHER SANDFORD

pitch

First published by Pitch Publishing, 2019

Pitch Publishing
A2 Yeoman Gate
Yeoman Way
Worthing
Sussex
BN13 3QZ
www.pitchpublishing.co.uk
info@pitchpublishing.co.uk



A CIP catalogue record is available for this book from the British Library.

ISBN 978 1 78531 487 2

Typesetting and origination by Pitch Publishing

Printed and bound in India by Replika Press Pvt. Ltd.

# CONTENTS

**Also by Christopher Sandford**

FICTION
*Feasting with Panthers*
*Arcadian*
*We Don't Do Dogs*

PLAYS
*Comrades*

MUSIC BIOGRAPHIES
*Mick Jagger*
*Eric Clapton*
*Kurt Cobain*
*David Bowie*
*Sting*
*Bruce Springsteen*
*Keith Richards*
*Paul McCartney*
*The Rolling Stones*

FILM BIOGRAPHIES
*Steve McQueen*
*Roman Polanski*

SPORT
*The Cornhill Centenary Test*
*Godfrey Evans*
*Tom Graveney*
*Imran Khan*

HISTORY
*Houdini and Doyle*
*Summer 1914*
*Macmillan and Kennedy*
*The Man Who Would be Sherlock*
*John F. Kennedy and Great Britain*
*The Zeebrugge Raid*
*Summer 1939*

To Colleen

# ACKNOWLEDGEMENTS

I BEGAN writing this book, with John Murray's guarded approval, in May 2018. I say 'guarded' because Murray didn't want it to be a statistical trawl through each and every one of his 635 first-class matches ('They'll fall asleep'), nor to linger too long over the biographer's traditional fetish for his subject's deprived childhood or troubled journey to the top. Instead, his advice was simple: 'Just give them an idea of what it was really like, and above all tell them how lucky I was.' I've tried to follow this excellent rule, and despite the news of 24 July 2018 I hope the reader won't find that the later chapters necessarily constructed from the material John left behind show any conspicuous falling off from the modest merits of the beginning.

In another sense I suppose I really began writing the book in around 1965, when as a star-struck eight-year-old I first became seriously obsessed with England's impossibly smooth wicketkeeper, and characteristically Murray himself always urged me to 'put some of your own spin' on the story. Again I've tried to follow his advice, while I hope not being wafted away on a haze of nostalgia or maudlin self-promotion. I was proud to call Murray my friend, and, while he unstintingly helped me with the book up until the day he died, neither he nor anyone else listed below can be blamed for the shortcomings of the text. They are mine alone.

There's a great deal to be said for the various places of education mentioned in this book. In spite of flaws more on my part than theirs, I actually enjoyed my time at the schools listed, and would like to particularly pay tribute to Mr Gervis (50 years later, it still seems impertinent to use a first name), Alan Kennington and Julian James at St Aubyns, and also to Dennis Silk, that fine amateur cricketer and impressively austere headmaster, who died in June 2019.

I would also particularly like to thank: Wendy Adams; Dave Allen; Pete Barnes; the late Richie Benaud; Rob Boddie; Emma Boycott; Geoff Boycott; Mike Brearley; Robert and Hilary Bruce; Jane Camillin; Paul Camillin; Alice Cooper; Ted Dexter; the late Godfrey Evans; Jon Filby; Steven Fletcher; Malcolm Galfe; Mary Gallivan; Ashley Giles; James Graham; the late Tom Graveney; Steve and Jo Hackett; Alex Holmes; Jo Jacobius; Imran Khan; Barbara Levy; Vince Lorimer; Robert Dean Lurie; Lee Mattson; Frank Misson; Colleen Murray; Nick Murray; Greg Nowak; Peter Parfitt; Robin Parish; Jim Parks; Peter Perchard; Clive Radley; Tim Rice; David Robertson; the late Sefton Sandford; Peter Scaramanga; Mike Selvey; Fred and Cindy Smith; John Snow; Garry Sobers; Jack Surendranath; Sussex CCC; the late Fred Titmus; Derek Underwood; Diana

Villar; Richard Whitehead; the Willis Fleming family; the late Aaron Wolf; and Yorkshire CCC. I'm grateful to Robin B. James for kindly supplying the book's index.

My deepest thanks, as always, to Karen and Nicholas Sandford.

C.S.
2019

*A man that fortune's buffets and rewards*
*Hast ta'en with equal thanks.*

– Hamlet, III. II

# 1.

# SUMMER OF LOVE

THE year 1967 was my own private summer of love, but not for any reasons connected with the world of herbally tinged joss sticks or bare-thighed young women swaggering around Carnaby Street in Courrèges miniskirts. You probably know the sort of retrospective that takes the Swinging Sixties, and more particularly Swinging London, on their own terms. 'Society was shaken to its foundations!' a recent BBC documentary on the subject shouted. 'All the rules came off, all the brakes came off ... the floodgates were unlocked ... A youthquake hit the UK', and so on.

For at least most young Britons, of whom I was one, what this mainly seems to have meant was some very silly shirts, marginally better food (thanks to new European trading laws) and, so one gathers, a slight increase in the use of soft drugs. By a lucky bit of timing, the introduction and rapid availability of the female contraceptive pill also happened to coincide with the arrival of that other defining symbol of swinging etiquette, the duvet. Exact statistics are elusive, but as a result of these twin developments it's likely that a few more single young women bunked up with their boyfriends, a societal trend celebrated in the Rolling Stones' seminal 1967 single 'Let's Spend the Night Together', one of several public effusions proposing nocturnal activity at around that time.

But in truth, that was about it for the youthquake. For millions of adolescent Britons, it seems fair to say that sex, drugs and rock 'n' roll took their place against a normal existence of knitting or cricket, with a probationary glass or two of Babycham, and worrying about one's school exams. A night out at *The Sound of Music*, followed by the Berni Inn Family Platter, remained the height of most young teenagers' aspirations. When *Time* magazine came to dub London the 'Style Capital of Europe', it focused on a few photogenic locations and eye-catching developments such as the pervasive rise of hemlines and Mick Jagger and Keith Richards appearing before magistrates on drug charges. Despite the subsequent claims of the BBC, these were not events that appeared to be part of any broader revolution under way against the Britain of *Hancock's Half Hour*, with its grinding conformity and identical, red-brick semi-detached houses furnished just like your granny's.

Certainly there was little evidence of anyone conspicuously seeking to move the guardrails defining the limits of acceptable behaviour to be seen at St Aubyns prep school in Rottingdean, East Sussex, where I found myself detained for much of 1967. Social ferment was slow to disturb that part of the world. The school itself was a combination of distressed seaside hotel and Victorian fortress, with innumerable outbuildings and corridors, all smelling obscurely of boiled cabbage, grouped around the central block, and a sturdy flint wall separating the whole place from a large, sloping playing field which sometimes made it feel like you were being pushed downhill when you were batting there. There was a road at the south end of the field, and beyond the road was the English Channel. In general it seems fair to say that St Aubyns wasn't known for its spirit of freewheeling social adventure. There was an elaborate system of rules, rewards and punishments, and the seven- to 13-year-old boys wore a year-round uniform of grey shirts and sweaters, and grey shorts, with an itchy grey suit by way of variety on Sundays and other special occasions. There were no girls. An etiquette of finely tuned call and response ruled between the students and the staff, the former known by our surnames, the latter answering to 'Sir'. There was something of a generation gap apparent in this relationship, and I suppose it could hardly have been otherwise in light of the fact that roughly half the dozen full-time masters had taught my father at the same institution 30 years earlier – 'and they seemed pretty ancient even then', he once told me.

As I say, though, there was love in the air during that summer of 1967, and in my case this meant cricket in general and more particularly the incumbent England wicketkeeper John 'JT' Murray. Murray was exquisite. The sheer class of the man communicated itself even on the boxy, black-and-white Baird TV set perched in a dim corner of the St Aubyns schoolroom where I principally watched him. He seemed to me to be much like Cary Grant with gauntlets. Always immaculately turned out in creamy white flannels and a blue cap, Murray would go through a little routine before each ball was bowled, circling his arms, the tips of the gloves touched together, patting the peak of the cap, and then dropping smoothly down to settle on his haunches behind the stumps. There was something both athletic and sedate about his posture. Murray's balance and coordination were such that he was hardly ever seen sprawled on the turf, though he could dive full length, making impossible catches seem simple, with the best of them. As *Wisden* wrote when honouring him as one of its Five Cricketers of the Year in 1967:

> 'Murray's reputation is built on polished orthodoxy and eschewing the spectacular for its own sake. He denies the need for flashiness … The sheer professionalism of his wicket-keeping has made an essential and vital difference to England's out-cricket.'

Murray could bat a bit, too. The sometime England captain Tony Lewis once wrote of him that he was the only player who could make hooking the West Indies fast bowlers of the 1960s (in the days before helmets) look positively graceful. At his best he was a glorious strokeplayer, as anyone who saw him take 112 off the likes of Wes Hall and Charlie Griffith in the fifth Test at the Oval in 1966 will confirm. Garry Sobers, who was there, told me: 'It was the rhythm and control John had that generated his power. When he got in a groove he was a bloody hard man to set a field to. "Just try and keep him up your end and bowl to the other bugger", I told Wes at one point, [but] that didn't work either – even the last-wicket pair, inspired by Murray, got runs that day.'

As the St Aubyns second eleven wicketkeeper, I sadly lacked these highly desirable attributes, and indeed brought only one recognisable quality to bear behind the stumps: being fat, I at least provided a generous target for the bowler to aim at. Murray was my idol, but he was in every sense an unapproachable one. I read the match reports in the newspaper every morning from cover to cover, entering JT's catches and other data for the season in a large blue-covered exercise book until the annual was concluded, at which point I started another one. This sometimes drew the scorn of those who didn't have cricket in the blood, but it's something any true lover of the game surely knows in their bones.

Looking back on it, there were two primary reasons for my hero-worship of the peerless Middlesex and England stumper. One of them was pleasure, and the other was escape. About 40 years later I found myself sitting at home in Seattle one morning watching a local news report about how 'ordinary Britons' were coping in the immediate wake of the 7/7 terrorist attacks, many of them apparently absorbed less by the television images of the outrages in London than by the progress of the one-day international being played between England and Australia at Leeds, and I see that I jotted in my diary: 'Cricket can be better than life.' Although I wrote this in 2005 I was only enshrining in print a slogan that had first dawned on me while watching John Murray go through his uniquely smooth and feline pre-delivery routine back on the communal TV set at St Aubyns.

In retrospect, I actually came pretty late to the table as a Murray devotee. Although the light of idolatry first flickered on for me around mid-1965, it was another two years before it attained its full voltage. It seemed to do so overnight. One aspect of our repressed national character, at least in my case, expresses itself in a tendency to go from relative indifference on a subject to one of total mania for it with no apparent transitional phase. Little did he or I know it, but by that heady summer of 1967 Murray was already embarking on his last season as England's first-choice wicketkeeper. In June he took six catches in a Test innings while playing against India at Lord's, thus equalling the world record set by Australia's Wally Grout ten years earlier. Yet just over a month later he was gone, axed in favour of the hyperactive if undeniably talented young Kent stumper, and affectionately known 'performing flea', Alan Knott. Anyone familiar with Jerry Lewis in his classic *The Nutty Professor* era need only think of that same character switching abruptly from the film's cool and composed Buddy Love to the twitchy and somewhat exhausting Julius Kelp, though without the prominent buck teeth, to get some of the flavour. That indignity stung a certain combative streak in Murray (not to mention a distinct pang in his admirers), and he spent the next year patiently scoring runs and bringing off dozens of impeccable catches and stumpings for Middlesex. It was one of the many ironies of his career that he hit some of the best form of his life immediately after the England selectors had dispensed with his services. Without descending too far into the briar-patch of individual playing records, it's perhaps worth noting that in the 1968 home season Murray and Knott each averaged around 25 with the bat and took 70 dismissals; in 1969 Murray averaged 30 to Knott's 21, while they managed 69 and 55 dismissals respectively. In this same period JT consistently stumped 15 or 20 batsmen a year, while Knott's tally was just nine or ten. But so much for statistics.

It wasn't until 1968/69 that Murray again caught the Test selectors' attention, and it was somehow in keeping with the roller-coaster trajectory of his international career as a whole that this was the occasion of the cancelled MCC tour of South Africa which fell victim of the host government's refusal to accept a multi-racial team chosen by what their state president characterised as 'troublemakers' in the anti-apartheid movement. In the event Knott kept in all three of the hurriedly-arranged replacement Tests in Pakistan, the last of which ended in some disarray when a crowd of some 4,000 disaffected students broke down the main gate of the National Stadium in Karachi, forcing play to be abandoned as riot police liberally doused the area with tear gas. Murray never represented England again. He had appeared in 21 Tests (the same total as Harold Larwood, and, for that matter, only one fewer than W.G. Grace, but still 112 less than Alec Stewart later managed) over the course of six years, and John Arlott spoke for many when he said that one way or another the selectors had treated him pretty shabbily, JT being the sort of keeper who was not only textbook-correct but also likely to do something truly brilliant at least once an innings. 'An occasional choice over the years looks odd because all the facts have not been broadcast or the particular needs of the Test fully aired,' Arlott acknowledged. 'But this was just bloody silly.'

Murray himself accepted triumph and adversity with the same stoic good cheer, apparently regarding it all as part and parcel of the professional sportsman's life. He continued to play for his native Middlesex until 1975, the year he turned 40, and it was another of the peculiar twists to his career that he subsequently, and unhappily, went on to serve as an England Test selector.

There were plenty of other admirable cricketers of Murray's vintage, of course, and several of them were more immediately recognisable household names even from behind the stone walls of St Aubyns. It wasn't that I was starved of possible alternative heroes. At the age of nine I could tell you the previous day's county championship bowling figures for Ken Higgs or John Snow, and describe in detail the all-round splendours irradiating from that exotic newcomer in our midst Basil D'Oliveira, or go on at some length about the distinct batting styles of Geoff Boycott, Colin Milburn or Tom Graveney, the last of whom later became a friend and in time the subject of a small book; but somehow there was no electrifying sense of personal identification with any of them, however grimly efficient or gaily inconsistent their individual merits. Graveney was the man I patronised. Murray was the man I worshipped. It was a great day for me when they both went out and flogged the West Indies bowling around the park on that sunny afternoon at the Oval in 1966.

In thinking over the part Murray has played in my life, I find myself dividing it into three phases. In the first phase it was a grand passion. In the second, the passion became a fondness in which, while still bulking large in my affections, Murray increasingly took his place among a backdrop of mullet-haired footballers and pop stars. In the third the grand passion stirred again, perhaps with a more nostalgic tone than before, and also tinged with a certain middle-aged perspective on the whole knotty business of fan worship. Because while Murray was undoubtedly my hero, he was also one of those engagingly flawed, or ill-starred, heroes whom the British seem to take to themselves. As Arlott again said, there was 'never the stamp of omnipotence or infallibility about his career', and here I think we come to the nub. Murray was what the author Christian Wolmar calls 'a nearly man', who should have played many more Tests than he did in the course of his 23-year professional career. Early on he had the misfortune to overlap with the inimitable Godfrey Evans, who was about as close as you could get to an automatic choice for the England Test side of the 1950s. In the middle years Murray came up against the new fad for picking wicketkeepers who could bat a bit rather than being the best specialist player in their position (and I might add in this context that Jim Parks himself once genially told me, 'John was a far better natural keeper than me'). And then just as Murray finally seemed to be getting the hang of it for England in the later 1960s the selectors traded him in for a new model, consigning him to the international junkyard at the age of 32. Which is all to say that a vein of disappointment appeared to run through JT's superficially glittering career, or even that, having arrived among us on April Fool's Day, he sometimes seemed to be the butt of some long-running cosmic joke.

As *Wisden* wrote about him in 1967:

> 'Long before the fates made atonement on late summer days at The Oval, 1966, there must

> have been times when John Thomas Murray was left with nothing more than a cricketer's natural philosophy as balm for his wounds. His career as England's wicket-keeper began on the highest note of promise with five Tests and five impeccable performances against Australia in 1961.
>
> 'None could have suspected his position would soon be assailed. Yet the first of his disappointments was round the corner. In the following winter of 1961/62 he had to return prematurely from MCC's tour of India and Pakistan to undergo an operation for varicose veins.'

After reviewing Murray's somewhat fitful Test career to date, *Wisden* added:

> 'The years of frustration did not leave a trace of bitterness. Nor was a word of complaint uttered. As No. 1 or No. 2 wicket-keeper in any touring side he pulled his weight cheerfully. He is immaculate in his turnout, and the key to his character is to be found in his own words: you have to try and do what is in the best interests of your side. That, in a nutshell, is JT Murray.'

* * *

*The Cricketer*'s letters page is an arena where the price of a plastic cup of beer at Lord's, the legal proceedings against certain England Test players and the suitability for office of Pakistan's current prime minister can all rub shoulders, so it's no surprise that not too long ago the magazine hosted a fascinating mini-debate on the perennial question: are all wicketkeepers mad? Most of the correspondents seemed to agree that they are. Leaving aside the claims of that irrepressible force of nature Godfrey Evans, who once worked off a hangover by taking a taxi direct from what he called a place of 'low entertainment' in London's West End to the England dressing-room at Lord's, enjoying a hurried breakfast of aspirin and a fat cigar, and then walking out to belt an unbeaten even-time 98 off a strong Indian attack, before somehow managing to set fire to his cricket coffin and much of the surrounding area during the lunch interval, but returning to the middle to polish off his century with a hooked four into the grandstand, and to concentrate instead on the modern breed: There was Knott himself, who perhaps set the bar with a range of idiosyncratic trademarks that included always keeping his shirt collar turned up to 'protect me from the sun', even on the most overcast days; his England successor Jack Russell, whose much-repaired floppy hat and wraparound shades were said to make him resemble a somewhat uneasy cross between the Terminator and Worzel Gummidge, with dietary fads that included the use of a stopwatch to time the soaking of his morning Weetabix, and who once seriously insisted that the builders coming to work on his home be blindfolded before they arrived and left so that they wouldn't know where he lived; and Russell's protégé Paul Nixon, whose sledging of the opposition wasn't so much limited to an occasional strategic barb as it was a non-stop running commentary touching on everything from the state of the weather to the batsman's parentage.

A few years earlier there was also Evans's contemporary at Kent, Hopper Levett, who after a heavy night once went out to take his place behind the wicket and never even blinked as the first ball sailed past the off stump for four byes.

The batsman had then glanced the second delivery down the leg side, where Levett took off to dive and take a spectacular catch, before turning to remark to the slip cordon: 'Not bad, eh, for the first ball of the day?'

These are very far from the only examples of the strange role the wicketkeeper often seems to perform as a sort of combined acrobat, custodian, *provocateur* and court jester in the typical cricket side. There's something indefinably but distinctly odd about the job. Suppose, for instance, the batsman pushes the ball towards point, and suppose there is no point, and suppose the keeper, being the nearest available first responder, hares off after the ball. What happens? Someone in the crowd will nudge someone else and start laughing. There's no logical reason why this should be so. The batsmen are also burdened with pads, gloves and helmets as they speed across the turf. No one laughs at them, unless of course they both happen to end up stranded at the same end. It's something about wicketkeepers. As a race they're not known for being shy, retiring types. It seems they're never short of a choice word or two, both on and off the field. It's said that at one time the Lancashire stumper George Duckworth had the loudest voice in England. They're just different. Aside from the levels of skill, athleticism and dedication that it takes to be a really top-flight keeper, it begins to look like a peculiarly masochistic if not suicidal position to want to occupy. Godfrey Evans once told me: 'You're squatting there with your view obscured as a guy runs in and bowls a bloody hard leather ball towards you, knowing there's a good chance you'll be smacked about a second later somewhere in your head, body or privates. If you relax for even an instant you're finished. In my first season I was playing twelfth man for Kent when Hopper Levett was keeper and I'd just put my feet up for a second when I heard the shout, "You're on, mate. They're bringing Hopper in on a stretcher." I went out and there were bits of teeth stuck in the grass behind the stumps.' I asked Evans why, under the circumstances, anyone would ever want to be a wicketkeeper. 'It's never boring,' he replied.

The strange thing about John Murray is that for much of the 1960s he managed to be both the world's greatest keeper and also, as his first Test captain Colin Cowdrey put it, 'the world's nicest man … There were quite a few high-maintenance characters in the England team in those days. You went out into the field and it was sometimes as though you were surrounded by a ring of children who all wanted your constant attention and got huffy if you saw more of one than the other … And John himself was the calm centre of this storm. I played with him on and off for about 20 years, home and away, and I remember him as always being cool and collected and agreeable, with a dry sense of humour, no matter what anyone else said or did. "You got money and your name put down for the MCC at birth from your parents," he told me one hot night in Lahore. "I got varicose veins."'

This was the superbly self-contained (as opposed to unambitious) and affable professional sportsman whom I worshipped as a boy and befriended as a man. Murray's basic social technique never varied in the 30 years or so of our adult meetings. As you got off the train at his home station he'd be standing by his car, whatever the weather, waiting for you with a broad grin on his face. You got a hearty, protracted handshake. He seemed to exude authority, not just power. He always enquired at length about you and your family before he talked about himself. I don't necessarily want to claim Murray was a father figure, but he certainly would have qualified as one of those friendly uncles who turned up from time to time to take you out to Sunday tea at St Aubyns and perhaps slip you a postal order as they were handing you back. He invariably seemed to know what you were up to. 'You're writing about Kurt Cobain, then, are you?' he asked out of the blue when he, Murray, was in his mid-sixties. 'Yes,' I said. 'Well, hope you go on with that,' he said, in a tone of warm encouragement I still remember.

About ten years later he sent me an email one morning: 'I read you today in the *Daily Mail*. Have told all the neighbours I know you. Could you autograph my book when you next come over?' From the very earliest days when I first saw him up close, a gawky schoolboy hanging around the pavilion door at Lord's, he displayed a remarkable gift for forging an instant connection with people he'd never met before. He was good company, a great listener, keenly attuned to the other party. In turn, you noticed Murray's rich baritone voice, his trim figure, sharp eyes, and slightly over-prominent teeth, like those of the Alec Guinness character in *The Ladykillers*. He was fundamentally light-hearted, given to bursts of excitement and deep enthusiasms which he communicated with a boyish passion. He laughed loudly and often.

In the sweltering summer of 1989 I was newly separated and living in a small flat in west London. The place had come furnished. It had little claim to elegance. The chairs and sofa were dipped in synthetic stain repellent. The rental agency supplied cooking utensils and bedding, which I thought it best to have industrially laundered on first taking possession. The previous tenant left me some Pam oven spray and Brut cologne.

One muggy night in late May there was a star-studded benefit dinner at the Grosvenor House Hotel for the great Lancashire and England bowler Brian Statham. We'll return to it in a later chapter, but suffice it to say they were all there that evening, from the papal figure of Jim Swanton with Gubby Allen on his arm down to the irrepressible Fred Trueman and my new friend Tom Graveney, then about 60, a deep-chested man of slightly less than average height with a jowly yet handsome face which had a built-in mischievous expression. You could see how he might once have fallen foul of the austere Len Hutton. Hutton was also there that night. He asked me for a cigarette just as we were sitting down to eat, a query followed by 'Then I'll smoke one of my own', and I remember him dragging away though much of the meal.

At the time I was writing a book about Godfrey Evans, who was then about to turn 70 but thanks to a pair of Dickensian mutton chop whiskers looked about ten years older. The great England stumper lived in somewhat makeshift circumstances in a friend's house in Northamptonshire, and as a result I sometimes put him up for the night when he was in town. (I got a rude shock when a boy hanging around my street in Hammersmith saw England's 1950s keeper come out of the front door with me one day, and later asked me with a straight face if we were perhaps brothers.) Anyway, I was sitting there opposite Hutton and between Evans and a nearly spherical Tony Lock, quite a lively spot, both of these last two cricketers increasingly making their points in a bellow and Lock, in particular, quite often punctuating his speech by swinging an arm – or two – high above his head or as an alternative pushing his hands up behind his ears and vigorously rubbing them there like a television commercial on headache misery. It was a long evening and, as I say, we'll return to it later. There was a table way back in the shadows of the ballroom, and as Evans and I later passed by it on our way out I noticed a slim, sparse-haired man in a dinner jacket sitting there with a mild, unassuming expression on his face that somehow contrasted with that of my recent companions. There was a moment of shocked recognition on my part, and then I remember asking Evans, in a strangulated voice, to introduce us. As he did so, he surprised me by giving one of those deep and I might add wholly unironic I'm-not-worthy bows before thrusting out a menu with the request, 'Can you sign this for my daughter, master?'

So there it was. Even to Evans, John Murray was the great wicketkeeper.

* * *

Murray himself did not particularly want to see this book in print. By that I don't for a moment mean that he actively opposed my plan to write it. No author has ever had a more sympathetic or genial subject than I did, and I speak from the wizened perspective of one with certain prior adventures in the field, including a brief but memorable rendezvous in the High Court over a libel writ, involving various brand-name rock and film stars. Writing about Murray after doing biographies of the likes of Cobain or Roman Polanski was refreshing; nobody threatened me with violence, or promised that I'd never work again, although I did once receive an enigmatic late-night phone message supposedly from a well-known former England all-rounder advising me never to contact him again, either on John Murray or any other possible subject, or else face the consequences. Perhaps it was all a joke.

So while Murray's initial response to my book proposal was unenthusiastic, his reservations didn't stem from him thinking himself too busy, or too grand, to help with the project. Just the opposite. The specific subject matter (as opposed to its wider cricket context) simply didn't appeal to him that much. Murray was the most genuinely modest and unaffected of all professional sportsmen. Literally scores of those I interviewed remarked on his simplicity and good manners, and said that whether on or off the field they'd enjoyed being around him – 'John had the priceless knack of always making you feel good,' Tom Graveney once told me.

Another colleague who also knew him socially added:

> 'John wasn't a monument to himself. He was a human being. He collected *Wisdens*. He went down the shops and did the gardening. He liked roast beef and a glass of plonk. I remember once he came home after taking a ton of catches for England, the hero of the hour, and at about nine o'clock that

> night I saw him coming out of the back of his place in north Wembley to put the rubbish bins out and line them up there in a neat row. *That* was JT.'

When the time came Murray was always the first man to congratulate a team-mate or to console an opponent. He invariably found the right words for the occasion. But people also noticed that he rarely seemed to speak about himself, and he kept his emotional distance – 'I don't know if he was really offering you friendship as much as friendliness,' a long-time Middlesex colleague told me, before adding: 'Nice as he was, he always kept things light. He once told me that I had a sensitive soul, and it was as if he was complimenting me on my golf swing.' Another team-mate who went into long-term therapy after he retired later came to believe that 'John had a permanent apparatus of self-containment' about him. 'There always seemed to be this slight reticence behind the supremely chummy façade.' Murray was shy about his achievements, much happier to share the credit for them with others, and laughed until he shook if reminded of some small technical lapse on his part of the sort other players might have preferred to forget or overlook. So it naturally took him a while to warm to the whole concept of someone writing a book about him – a project no one had seriously suggested during the previous 40 years – and, equally characteristically, when the time came no one could have ended up being more open and generous to me than he was. John gave me dozens of informal interviews, often conducted late at night around his dining room table, and always cheerfully answered every question I asked him. On the last occasion we met, he handed me a box containing several bundles of old contracts, letters and other mementoes of his playing days, saying only of this precious cargo, 'I don't know if this lot would be any use to you?' There was just one exception to this otherwise free-spirited and unstinting gift of his time and treasure, and that came when I once asked him if by any chance he happened to have a childhood photograph he might be willing to lend to the cause, and he replied evenly, 'Sorry. We were too poor ever to own a camera.'[1]

Somehow that seemed only fitting in prefiguring the life of a world-class sportsman who preferred to shun the personal limelight to a degree unusual in our self-obsessed age. John Murray was a great wicketkeeper. He was also 'a wonderfully sane, down-to-earth bloke, who kept smiling even when the selectors buggered him about', said Tom Graveney, who added: 'Every team-mate liked him and every opponent respected him.'

Who could ask for a better epitaph than that?

---

1 One boyhood picture finally came to light, and is included in the book.

# 2.

# 'MY MONEY IS ON MURRAY'

OUTWARDLY, John Murray seemed enamoured of the glamour and prestige of being a first-class cricketer of his day, and he saw to it that his public conduct never betrayed any inner doubts he might possibly have had on the subject. He was not only the most technically refined English player of his generation but, with the possible exception of 'Lord Ted' Dexter, about the smoothest too. I regret to say that at least part of Murray's appeal to me, a febrile nine-year-old at my Victorian prep school, was on the social level; there was a small but perceptible snobbish element in the choice of my principal idol, although in my defence I might add that better judges than me were also similarly struck by the suave and debonair manner with which Murray approached his duties. 'When John came in to bat no one quite knew whether to bow, shake his hand, or just set the field,' Richie Benaud once told me. 'And it was like having God himself standing behind you when he kept wicket. As far as the Australians knew, he might have been wafted down from Mt Olympus.'

In fact John Murray hailed from the slightly less exalted surroundings of north-west London, in a council home bordered by Wormwood Scrubs prison on one side and the White City dog track on the other – not far from the scene of the later Grenfell Tower tragedy – arriving among us on the wet Monday morning of 1 April 1935. It was the era of Stanley Baldwin, German rearmament and lectures on the Responsibility of Youth – 'You will have to sacrifice much while others fight to repair a troubled and broken world' was how he summarised the standard school speech of the late 1930s. John's father Jim was the son of a Hammersmith borough stonemason, and apparently never quite found his own place in the world. Most accounts describe him as a charming but rather weak man whose consuming goal in life was to hold down a corporation job with an old-age pension attached to it. He finally achieved this ambition but then died at 58, too young to reap the benefits. John Murray remembered his father as 'a restless man, professionally a nobody, who used to make a few extra bob by helping out my Uncle John as a bookmaker at Kempton Park or Epsom. He had a good head for numbers.' There was another uncle, Charlie, who operated as a bookie's runner, and one or two cousins in the same general trade who 'occasionally had to leg it from angry punters'. John's boyhood does not seem to have been that much of a *Brideshead*-like idyll. His mother Florence worked on the production line at the giant Lyon's bakery factory in Hammersmith, and like millions of other families the Murrays had a salutary struggle to make ends meet in the depths of the Depression. 'Neither of my parents were very well or very happy in life,' John recalled. He had both an older and a younger sister, and was a bit cagey when I pressed him further about his early years. 'They were happy enough,' he said, 'but bloody hard graft, too, at times.' I asked him if his father, who died in 1958, had been proud to have lived to see his only son playing professionally at Lord's. 'Up to a point,' said Murray, guardedly. 'His last ever words to me were: "You're having a bit too much fun in life, son."'

John Murray's first contact with formal education, at the Latimer Road School in Hammersmith, came as something of a mutual shock. Today a maze of gastropubs, one-way systems, speciality shops and subsidised flats (a relic of the moment in 1977 when squatters declared the area the 'Republic of Festonia', and the red flag fluttered atop the current site of the Royal Kensington and Chelsea pupil support centre), in the 1940s the neighbourhood had few pretensions to opulence. One commentator had written of the area just a few years earlier: 'Between Notting Hill and Wormwood Scrubs lies a vast desert of human dwellings ... by scarcely perceptible degrees, there is a declension of so-called respectability, till at last the frankly working-class district of Latimer Road is reached.' In Murray's day the immediate area around the school had a large industrial laundry to one side and an urban pigsty to the other, both of which 'niffed a bit', John remembered, when the wind blew a certain way. 'I wasn't much of a student,' he added.

Murray's early education also coincided with the worst ravages of the war on the home front. The Latimer Road school remained open with a skeleton staff during the hostilities, and the London *Evening News* of 1943–44 conveys some of the terror of everyday life: 'Flying Bombs Night and Day ... Parents, Daughter and Cook Killed ... Old Station Blasted ... Child Killed Running for Cover ... Tragedy of Two Brothers'. The Murrays kept brown tape stuck over their windows, and made an improvised fallout shelter under the kitchen table. They had neither a car nor a fridge, and only a two-bar electric fire in their front room that gave off about as much heat as a 60-watt light bulb. The family shopped every day within the limits of their ration at the local United Dairies or Mr Hook the Butcher. There were sometimes boiled sweets for the children, and on birthdays the almost Babylonian luxury of a Mars Bar, which was ceremonially cut up into five small slices. John remembered that there'd also been a 'modest booze-up' somewhere in or around the street most weekends, and that 'you never knew if it would be the last one before you copped it'. On the night of 22 June 1944 a German V1 bomb landed on a house two doors along from the Murrays, and killed the family of six who lived there.

In September 1946, the beginning of the most miserably cold and wet winter in living memory, Murray entered the nearby St John's School in Sirdar Road. 'I was still a dud academically,' he admitted cheerfully. But sometime in the following, gloriously warm summer, when Denis Compton and Bill Edrich were in full sail and England were beating South Africa 3-0 in the Test series, the 12-year-old first picked up a cricket bat in anger. 'I was pretty good,' he allowed, for once casting modesty aside. Oddly enough, Murray, while not yet known for his work in the field, was also a better than average seam bowler. Coming in off a short run, with a fast arm, his 'windmill' delivery baffled the schoolboy hitters whose repertoire ran largely to the prod or the slog. They never could get a good look at the ball, and by the time they did see it it was often obscured by the clump of tall trees immediately behind the bowler's arm. There were no sight screens, and precious few other amenities, at the Sirdar Road ground. Nobody had yet mentioned anything about John becoming a wicketkeeper.

Murray was also a boxer in his teenaged years. He had 14 official fights and even made it to the final of the English Schoolboy Championships, where he went down to a local bruiser named Herby Fraser. In another contest he was up against an opponent advertised only as The Beast, but whose real name was Cyril Capes. When they touched gloves before the bell, he told Murray in a slightly curious locution: 'I'm going to smear you all over the ring till you're marmalade.' The Beast seemed to get stronger as the bout continued. In the sixth round he threw a sudden flurry of punches to the body and then another brutal haymaker to the head. Murray went out with the lights. 'That finished me as a fighter,' he said.

Soon Murray was regularly walking the three miles to and from Lord's, where he saw something of Don Bradman's legendary 1948 Australians. He'd caught the cricket bug. We know now that John clung hard to his adolescent dreams of glory, including the seemingly unattainable one of becoming a professional sportsman. His family and boyhood contemporaries weren't aware of this fact. 'They probably thought I'd end up in the army, if not something a bit dodgy,' he recalled. The Murrays were an eminently respectable family, but they moved in colourful circles. A couple of years later John was on the groundstaff at Lord's, where his duties sometimes included carrying a bag full of the day's box office takings across the road to Barclays Bank in nearby St John's Wood High Street. 'One afternoon I was walking out the top gate with a couple of hundred quid in a tatty old shopping bag, and there was my old family pal Freddie "Fingers" Robinson strolling past. I hadn't seen him in a while. We stopped to chat, and I asked him what he'd been up to. He told me he'd just done three years in the Scrubs for armed robbery.'

By 1949 Murray was appearing as an all-rounder both for his school and the Rugby Boys Club sides. The latter had their own field, bomb-scarred but playable, across the road from the main corporation cemetery in North Acton. Archie Fowler, an occasional Middlesex left-arm spinner who, like Murray, was born on April Fool's Day (although in 1891, not 1935) served as head coach. Despite its irregularities, the pitch at Acton was usually full of runs. With big hitting practically always a factor the wide open spaces there could toy with the fielders, making them look like so many cats chasing a cricket ball-shaped laser light. Fowler evidently saw something he liked in Murray's batting, because he wrote: 'You are a natural talent and considering the tempo of your career, are well on the way to the possibility of playing at the top table. Just keep your head screwed on,' he added.

Murray was ready to make a go of it that same year, but then the school-leaving age was raised to 15. Around the time he was listlessly sitting a few final exams, the grand old man of Middlesex and England cricket, Pelham Warner, wandered on to the park at Acton one Saturday afternoon. 'It was like having Sir John Gielgud come to your local village Christmas panto,'

Murray recalled. On top of his many other accomplishments, Warner (an old Rugby man) had recently served as manager of the de facto England side in the West Indies – a role he'd also performed on the Bodyline tour of 1932/33 – and soon went on, at the age of 76, to be elected president of the MCC. He was also a practising journalist, a Test selector, and the reigning *eminence grise* at Middlesex. All in all, 'Plum's opinion was only slightly less exalted at Lord's than the voice of God,' E.W. Swanton wrote.

Warner watched Murray score an even-time 82 that afternoon, and then came back to see him add a century and take four quick wickets in an action-packed week in west London that also saw Middlesex narrowly beat Derbyshire in their last home fixture of the season and thus win a share of the county championship. The great man called John aside after the second match. Might this be the moment for a genial word of congratulation, the teenager wondered, or perhaps even some priceless technical advice on the part of a man who had played 15 Tests and over 500 first-class matches during the course of a 26-year career, and who now lived in a mansion flat in South Kensington watched over by a former county colleague and ex-soldier with one arm, the living room of which was decorated by a run of canary-yellow *Wisden*, a grandfather clock in the shape of a wicket, and original Spy cartoons framed on the walls?

Not quite. 'You're acceptable,' Warner announced. 'You'll be hearing from us.'

On the dank Monday morning of 3 April 1950, Murray got off the tube at St John's Wood in high spirits and walked through the north gate at Lord's to officially join the MCC groundstaff. He had turned 15 just two days earlier, and any illusions he may have had about becoming a professional cricketer were rapidly dispelled when the ground supervisor, a Pickwickian old stager named Leslie Symes, simply handed him a broom and told him to get on with it. Four hours later John sat down to eat his brown-bag lunch on an old section of bench he found stowed away in a corner of the shed where they kept the mowers by the clerk of the works' office. Within seconds he could feel the wooden seat collapsing beneath him. He landed on top of a pile of old grass cuttings with his legs pointing into the air and bleeding from his hand and knees. He also had a rip in his trouser leg and grime all over his new white cricket sweater. It turned out the bench had recently been retired because its planks had been all but eaten through by damp, or 'rotted to buggery', as Leslie Symes cheerfully put it. Symes himself came in to investigate when he heard all the commotion. He didn't even blink on seeing his new apprentice lying on his back covered in blood. 'Hard luck,' he muttered.

Murray never complained about the more menial aspects of his two probationary years at Lord's. In that first season he played just one three- or four-hour game of cricket a week, and that was the only time he was actually allowed in the pavilion. He was just glad to be there, working amongst all the props familiar to the lower reaches of English professional sport: deckchairs, oily, backfiring lawnmowers, tiny plastic cups of volcanic tea, and a sparse but surprisingly loyal fan base who turned up most mornings when there was a match to watch the young prospects go through their paces on the Nursery Ground. Aside from the Dickensian figure of Symes himself, there was something agreeably archaic about the whole routine.

Murray told me:

> 'You were either "A" staff or "B" staff. That was the big distinction. The "A" boys were always on call to play cricket. "Lord Muck's here, and he wants a net", Symes would announce, and there'd be a race to be the first out the door. You could do pretty well for yourself as a net bowler in those days. One old boy always put a ten-bob note down on the stumps, and you kept it if you hit them. It was a bit different for those of us down the "B" list. Basically you were sweeping and painting, and on match days you were also flogging scorecards. They cost 3d and you got a farthing commission for each one you sold. It added up. I made about 15 quid that way in the 1950 season.'

In 1951, Murray progressed successively from the 'B' staff to the 'A' staff, then to playing for the Lord's Nippers XI, then the Club and Ground side, and finally to the Middlesex second eleven. He was short and slight of build at 16, and he quite often got hit about the head or body when batting against the bigger fast bowlers. No one thought about chest protectors or helmets in those days. 'I had a little schoolboy's box and a pair of pads that looked like they'd done service in W.G. Grace's day,' Murray remembered. On 20 June of that year he went out to bat in his second eleven debut away to Essex, and a burly seam bowler in his mid-thirties named Lindsey Jerman yorked him first ball. 'Not a good start,' John admitted.

Even so, it wasn't a completely inauspicious introduction to top-level cricket. In between innings, the Middlesex captain and sometime stumper Tony Kamm, late of the Boys' Club, strolled up and said casually: 'Glove up, John. My hand's knackered, and you're keeping.'

Although unexpected, the idea of becoming a wicketkeeper wasn't without a certain appeal for Murray. He may not have known much about the role per se – despite one previous experience in a game at Acton – but he did know about the art of catching a cricket ball. He was quick and light on his feet, and along with thousands of other impressionable English adolescents of the day he idolised the great Test keeper Godfrey Evans. Like Evans, Murray enjoyed being at the centre of things. So when the summons came, he uncomplainingly put on his captain's outsize gauntlets, tried a couple of test squats and shadow takes in front of the cracked dressing-room mirror and, as he later said, 'just got on with it'. He was a natural. In the Essex second innings Murray brought off a catch and two stumpings, conceding a total of four byes off a ball that hit a crack and bounced again only when halfway back to the pavilion. Towards the end the Middlesex fast right-armer Reg Deller sent one down that nipped off the seam, clipped the edge of the batsman's pad-buckle and flew down the leg side. Murray took off like a bird in flight and caught it. Tony Kamm, standing down at third man, walked up at the end of the over and told John: 'You may never make a better stop than that.' At the close of play, Kamm added: 'Get used to it, mate. I've just retired.'

Murray always wore his fame lightly, and when he went home to White City that night and they asked him how he'd gotten along against Essex he said only 'All right', and that was the last anyone had heard about it until they read the match report in the following Saturday's *Sporting Life*. John was back behind the stumps against the Sussex seconds, at Enfield, a few days later. The visitors' left-handed all-rounder Ron Willson would go on to a distinguished playing career both at home and abroad, later appearing alongside Basil D'Oliveira when the latter made his debut in a game between an International XI and Rhodesia at Kitwe in Zambia. But more to the point, Willson was also the first batsman ever to depart with the notation against his name in the scorebook *c Murray b Titmus*, a significant harbinger of things to come. This particular partnership was one of the major factors that combined around 1951 to transform a high-grade teenaged hopeful into an artist whom even E.W. Swanton was willing to call 'serious'.

The off-spinning Fred Titmus, the son of a London railwayman, was then aged 18 and had already passed into cricket lore with the wonderfully hierarchical p.a. announcement at Lord's: 'For F. J. Titmus on your scorecard, please read Titmus F.J.' He went on to take an astonishing 2,830 first-class wickets in a 33-year professional career that began when Clement Attlee was in office and ended during the premiership of Margaret Thatcher. Short, compact and beetle-browed, chirpy as a cockney sparrow, Titmus kept up a non-stop flow of chatter while in the field, sometimes continuing a muttered discussion with a team-mate or opponent while actually in the process of bowling. He lost four toes in a boating accident on England's tour of the West Indies in 1967/68, but never his line and length. A batsman generally had to take risks against him if he wanted to score runs, because he would otherwise have to wait a long time for a loose delivery.

For all that, Titmus was not an easy man to keep wicket to. For one thing, he bowled straight as often as he really turned the ball, and for some reason there was never a really satisfactory system in place to signal to the keeper what to expect next. He also did most of his bowling at Lord's, where thanks to the ridge the bounce was notoriously uneven. The qualities that designated the place as the headquarters of cricket didn't always extend to the excellence of its pitch. 'After the sun had been on it a few days, the Lord's wicket was like a trampoline,' Murray once remarked. Titmus typically took just a couple of quick, shuffling steps and simply floated the ball down towards the right-hander's outside edge. Naggingly persistent rather than truly penetrative, no spinner has ever made more of his relatively modest natural talents. He and Murray hit it off immediately. 'Fred would bowl 20 or 30 overs in a day, then he'd drag me into the nets and say, "Is my arm too low?" or, "Am I getting too square on?" He was the ultimate professional. Not a bad bloke down the pub, either.'

Murray made his first-class debut on Saturday, 24 May 1952, the first day of Middlesex's away match with Leicestershire. He had turned 17 just the month before, and it was barely five years since he first played cricket on a semi-organised basis. Jack Robertson and Denis Compton both scored centuries for the visitors, who were on their way to fifth place in that season's championship table. Murray scored three in his first innings, caught the Leicester and future England batsman Gerry Smithson, missed another sharp chance standing up, and was said by *Sporting Life* to have turned in a 'very respectable overall show'. *The Times* thought 'young Murray did far more right than wrong' and 'displayed wicketkeeping [which] was always high class'.

Other reviews were not so favourable. There was a total of 40 byes or leg-byes in the two Leicester innings, and one critic thought Murray was 'still sometimes weak when taking to the spinners', though he was 'generally neat and agile standing back'. Obviously he wasn't yet the finished article. Mike Brearley came in to the Middlesex side in 1961, and remembers that by then there was 'no better model than JT [of how] to catch the ball – fingers down, hands relaxed, a long easy "give" to one side or other of the body'. We can probably settle on 1957 as the season marking Murray's full flowering as a top-flight technical wicketkeeper-batsman. He managed 1,025 first-class runs and 104 dismissals (23 of them stumpings) that year, making him only the second ever man, after Les Ames of Kent and England, to the fabled wicketkeeper's double.

At 17, Murray was dapper, good-humoured and outwardly self-confident. He was welcome wherever he went. He never said anything unpleasant about anyone, and appeared to have slipped in to professional cricket almost without conscious effort. Much of this was a front. It was all about presentation, he once admitted: how you looked, how you held yourself, how you responded in adversity, or when shaking with nerves. Overnight, it seemed, he was playing with men whose boots he'd been content to shine just a few weeks earlier. 'There's a big difference between being a useful schoolboy cricketer and playing the game with the grown-ups,' he later remarked, with typical understatement. 'It was a huge leap forward in every department, particularly since

Middlesex still thought I should score runs.' Generally happiest when playing fast bowling, Murray's bat could seem glued to the crease against the spinners. He managed to score only 17 and nought in his next match for Middlesex, against Cambridge University, who admittedly had the South African Test bowler Cuan McCarthy in their ranks. He fared better the following week against Kent at Lord's, with four catches and an unbeaten 43 in the second innings. Middlesex's captain on the day Bill Edrich said 30 years later: 'There are strapping great kids who flit in and out of a side, then disappear, and there are others you look at and say, he's not just a cricketer, he's a thinker ... John was like that. He used his loaf. He was just 17, but he'd figure the opposition batsman out. He'd look the bloke in the eye and then sidle up to you in between overs: "That bugger fancies himself against the short stuff. Give him a bouncer." You'd do that, and sometimes the ball would sail over the fence, but more often than not he'd hit it straight down the fielder's throat.'

I asked Murray what the atmosphere had been like in a Middlesex dressing-room not short of outspoken personalities. There was Edrich himself, for example, his upturned nose giving him a vaguely feral air ('like a randy mole', in one wife's assessment) who listed his chief pursuits in life as 'food, drink, sport and women', though it's not known if he gave these enthusiasms in any particular order of precedence. Having survived three years' wartime combat duty as an RAF bomber pilot, the Middlesex all-rounder tended to live for the moment. This policy had perhaps reached its apogee on the rest day of the Test against the West Indies at Old Trafford in 1950, when Edrich had returned to the team hotel late at night, depending on whose account you believe, either by the expedient of shinning up a rear drainpipe outside his window, or by enlisting the aid of the hall porter to carry him up the stairs. In either case, it seems fairly certain that he'd woken up the occupant of the next room, who happened to be Bob Wyatt, the chairman of selectors, and that this had disastrous consequences for his future career. Despite scoring nearly 2,000 first-class runs that season, Edrich was duly missing from the winter's MCC tour of Australia. It's been said that his favourite pastime was 'getting married and divorced with metronomic regularity', and that his numerous intervening trysts tended to be brisk: 'He didn't even take his cricket boots off,' one lady later sighed.

Impressive as all this was, Edrich wasn't alone among his Middlesex team-mates when it came to seizing the day or speaking his mind. There was also the likes of 35-year-old Jack Robertson, a Dunkirk veteran, later capped 11 times by England; the young Yorkshireman Don Bennett, who combined cricket with appearing as a titanically aggressive full-back for Arsenal; and the 21-year-old swing bowler Alan Moss, who on his day could run through a team, often exchanging pleasantries with each departing batsman as he did so. None of these individuals was exactly a martyr to false modesty. Looming over them all was the legendary Denis Compton, then aged 34 and just embarking on the Late Period of a glittering career that had already seen him win some 50 England caps, and led John Arlott to rhapsodise of his batting in the sun-kissed summer of 1947: 'To close the eyes is to see again that easy, happy figure at the wicket, pushing an unruly forelock out of the eye … never again will the boyish delight in hitting a ball with a piece of wood flower so directly into charm and gaiety and all the wealth of achievement.'

More to the point as far as Murray was concerned, Compton's elder brother Leslie appeared 272 times for Middlesex from 1938–56, often playing as wicketkeeper. A large man, he dominated the crease by bulk rather than excessive subtlety or technique. The older Compton was already on his way out with a chronically bad back by 1952, and he would have been less than human not to feel a certain twinge of animus towards the fresh-faced teenager taking his place. Murray assured me that 'Les was very dignified' and 'cut an elegant figure: wavy black hair, big and strong, calm in the face of adversity, always gracious in interactions with others in public and private situations, and never displaying less than good manners in the field.' He paused for a moment after this encomium. 'I think of the two brothers, Denis was probably more uptight about seeing this new kid behind the stumps,' he added. 'I remember there was an incident in that first match against Leicestershire. I'd seen this trick Godfrey Evans did while keeping for England where he'd take the ball and then flick it out of the side of his hands to Denis, at first slip, without turning to look at him. Well, I tried that. Denis wasn't expecting it and the ball ricocheted off the side of his head. Very bitter about it, he was. "You're not fucking Godfrey Evans, and don't forget it," he said. We eventually became good mates after that.'

One other thing about Murray's developing finesse behind the stumps. Over the years, the little routine he went through before each ball of swinging his arms and patting the tips of his fingers together before assuming the position won a sort of cult following all of its own. It was always a particular thrill to watch him briskly sweep his white-backed gauntlets around, almost as if he were playing air piano, and one critic wrote of the whole performance: 'This endlessly repeated drill could have served no material purpose, but rather stands as one of those superfluous rituals at once preparatory, confirmatory or transitional in an athlete's innate or conditioned motor behaviour.'

Murray himself had a more prosaic explanation. 'The ruddy gloves were always too loose on my hands, so I tapped them to tighten them up,' he said.

Compton and Edrich took turns captaining Middlesex in 1952, which meant that the eminent if underachieving London club (Surrey going on to win the first of their seven consecutive titles) was led by two of the most gloriously anti-establishment cricketers on the circuit, each with a track record of flouting rules, breaking curfews, and appearing at breakfast dressed in the previous night's dinner jacket. (Edrich took on the job unilaterally in 1953.) 'It was all good fun in its way,' said Murray. 'But you wouldn't confuse it for a modern professional sports outfit. There was never any sort of team meeting. Denis and Bill were both great players, but let's just say they didn't exactly fire on all cylinders when they happened to be somewhere like Buxton or Ashby-de-la-Zouch on a wet Wednesday morning. Neither of them ever talked about having "a strategy" or "sharing a vision". You never heard anything about therapists or dieticians. We trained on cheese sandwiches and fags. If you got hurt, an old boy might show up to the dressing-room and hold an army-surplus sun-lamp over you. Otherwise, you just got on with it.'

Like many other professional English cricketers of the day, Murray also played competitive football. He turned out several times in midfield for the Brentford youth team, and played one match against a Manchester United side that included 16-year-old Duncan Edwards. (Brentford lost.) Murray was in bed one Sunday morning at the family's new terraced home in Mersey Street, since destroyed to make way for the Hammersmith Flyover. 'Get up, you lazy sod,' his father suddenly hissed at the door. 'Tommy Lawton's downstairs.' The legendary centre forward, scorer of 22 goals in his 23 England appearances, now winding down his career as player-manager at Brentford, had come to offer professional terms. 'I leapt out of bed, threw on grey flannels and a blue blazer, and ran down to the front room. There was Lawton. My father idolised him. They offered me a fiver a week, and I thought about it, but in the end I chose cricket. Dad wasn't unhappy with the decision.'

That wasn't quite the end of Murray's football career, however. In the winter of 1952/53 he was still training with Brentford while turning up for a token net organised by Middlesex in a porous-roofed shed of military décor tacked on to the back of Alexandra Palace. Subsidence from wartime bomb damage meant that the artificial turf there sloped perceptibly from one side to the other, which was at least good practice when it later came to playing at Lord's. Murray's perfectionism drove him on. He was happy to talk to me about the rudimentary approach most cricketers then took to their physical fitness, and about players who slacked off. 'I always turned up, no matter how sick I was,' he noted. 'I buggered up my hand early one season, probably '56, cut it and it got infected, blew up like a balloon. Now' – he went on to explain the problem to me – 'for a wicketkeeper, having a hand that can actually catch the ball is quite important. It's the basic minimum. So I had to go out in front of a big Whitsun Saturday crowd at Lord's and play with this great red claw, the size of a frying-pan, that wouldn't close. Not ideal for a stumper.'

I was sympathetic. 'That had to be a dangerous situation. Taking to someone like Alan Moss would be hard enough for a man with two good hands.'

Murray nodded.

'Before I went out the old boy came up from the physio's room and gave me a numbing shot in my palm that made it even worse. He looked like something out of a Hammer horror film, a little hunchbacked bloke with wild eyes and a ruddy great horse syringe in his hand. But I wanted to play, you see? That was my whole life in those days.'

When I asked Murray what the outcome had been, he told me he thought he'd done 'all right' but couldn't remember the details. I looked them up. Middlesex v Sussex at Lord's, May 1956: J.T. Murray took four catches in the one Sussex innings on a wicket of 'erratic bounce', and then went out to open the Middlesex batting. He scored 9, which was low, admittedly, but still more than any of the middle-order specialists managed. *The Times* report added that he showed 'immaculate glovework', with that 'engaging air of utter composure' he brought to the 'heaviest and most trying of challenges'.

* * *

Within a few weeks of his 18th birthday in the coronation year of 1953, Murray had signed up for national service with the RAF, was issued with a wool uniform ('it weighed about

20 pounds when it was wet'), and found himself posted as a lowly aircraftsman, 2nd class, to a base at Innsworth, near Gloucester. This all came as something of a shock, as it would for any young man just breaking himself in as a professional cricketer. But the basic routine grew more congenial over time. RAF Innsworth then housed some 5,000 personnel, three-quarters of them from the women's branch of the service. There were 'social advantages' to this, Murray allowed. It was also home to a large cookery school, meaning that the new recruit spent most of his working hours in the rations store 'hauling great slabs of meat or bags of spuds around from A to B. The highlight of the week was always four o'clock sharp on a Friday afternoon, when the CO's car pulled up at the back door. We loaded him up with all his grub for the weekend, and in return we always had a pass for a couple of days' leave whenever we wanted it. I got two quid a week from the RAF and another two quid a week as a retainer from Lord's. There wasn't a lot left over,' Murray recalled, and added: 'Let's just say some of the lads supplemented their income in various ways.' The *Gloucester Citizen* of August 1953 seems to speak to this fact when it records a sorry fall from grace in its tale of two individuals who had appeared in court charged with selling hocks of ham 'for stewing or braising purposes', knowing these to have been 'wrongfully obtained from non-civilian personnel', each of them to be handed a ten-bob fine. Although Murray was always hard pressed to make ends meet while in the RAF, there was no suggestion that he was tied up in this scandal.

* * *

Murray used some of his extensive down-time from Innsworth playing for the Middlesex second eleven, for whom he had a number of individual successes: four catches in an innings against Northants seconds, three more and a stumping in a charity game with the touring Australians. He was still opening the innings and scoring a few runs (including a career-best unbeaten 74 against Kent), but after suffering the indignity of a king pair away to Essex he started dropping further down the order.

Murray nonetheless appeared as a specialist batsman for the Combined Services in 1954, hitting 71 against a full-strength Pakistani touring side at Catterick. There was plenty of festival or inter-forces cricket at the weekends. He also managed to get in as many as nine or ten matches against the first-class counties each summer. Life in uniform was in many ways less of an ordeal for him than it might have been for a non-sportsman. The main problem was the boredom that set in each September, the sheer repetition of it all, and that sinking Sunday-evening feeling that came over him, as it did many other Britons of the era, when it was time to walk back to Paddington in the rain and get in the third-class compartment of a train returning him to base. As a rule John's mother kissed him goodbye on these occasions and said 'Be a good boy. Remember to write,' and his father, who took a dim view of youth culture (this was the season of Bill Haley and the definitive teen-rebel film *Blackboard Jungle*), looked at him critically and announced, 'You're a bit of a lad, aren't you? Just keep your trousers on.'

Murray separated from the RAF with an honourable discharge on 19 August 1955, at a time when the papers were full of Anthony Eden's new Tory government, the hanging of Ruth Ellis for shooting her unfaithful lover, and what the *Evening News* called the 'half-gibberish and lunatic ravings' of a French-language play that premiered on the English stage as *Waiting for Godot*. A day later, John was back in civvies playing for Middlesex against Surrey at Lord's. He was victimless for once, but going in at number six scored a solid 26 and 22. Surrey won by nine wickets. Denis Compton was still in the Middlesex side, and seemed to have forgiven Murray for the *faux pas* of hitting him on the head while in the field three years earlier. I once asked Compton what had stood out about JT in those days.

'Balance,' he said. 'John kept absolutely still until it was time for him to move. Not all keepers do that. They're hopping around behind the stumps like a jack-in-the-box. But not JT. He was always calm and relaxed, and in five years I never once saw him twitch a muscle until he'd suddenly jump up out of the chorus line to catch the ball or whip off the bails for a swift stumping.' Compton rubbed in this plot development by adding: 'He really had the footwork of a ballet dancer, and I mean that in the best possible sense. You knew just by seeing him there, perfectly poised to leap out, that he was a class act. He was always attractive to watch, whether he was keeping or batting, and the crowd loved him. Bought his round, too.'

* * *

Godfrey Evans, about whom there was perhaps more a touch of the bustle than in Murray, was still a near-automatic choice as England's wicketkeeper in 1956. There were those who thought Evans, at 35, just past his peak, and others who felt he was never quite the same after breaking several bones in his hand in a Test the previous summer against South Africa. But in the normal course of events he remained the man in possession. Murray was still just 21, and his only immediate ambition was to win his county cap. Before the start of the new season Bill Edrich told him: 'Your target is 50 victims. Do that and I'll see you right.' It was the proverbial moment of clarity. 'They were still buggering around with me as an opener,' Murray recalled, 'and I told Bill: drop me down the order for good, and let me concentrate on wicketkeeping.' Murray finished with 77 first-class dismissals, more than any other English keeper, and duly won his cap. He was attracting press comment too. John Arlott wrote, 'He looks young and vigorous, possesses all the attributes of a possible future Test performer, [with] that ability to appear both fast on his feet and yet completely unhurried. This last art you will, I think, find only in the best players.' Even the venerable Neville Cardus thought Murray 'a thoroughly good prospect'.

Fifty years later, Murray began to talk about some of the less glamorous facts of life as a young first-class cricketer, although he was always quick to acknowledge that it was 'all a lot better than sweating away as a council labourer or a box-packer on the Lyon's production line'. He described a daily routine it would be hard to imagine a county professional accepting with any equanimity today, and how his reputation for always turning out on parade looking like one of those bygone Corinthian figures with a foppish cut to their blazer and razor-sharp creases to their flannels was all down to a combination of residual RAF discipline, and to first his mother and then his wife lovingly washing and ironing all his self-bought kit each night in the modest front room of the family's west London semi. Still, they were good times.

'When you travelled around the circuit it was a case of hitching a lift with someone like Compo, who had a car, or else going up by train. The junior pro, often yours truly, would handle all the players' gear and get this mountain of kit into a couple of taxis and up to Euston, or wherever it was, then unload it all again at the other end and deliver everything to the team hotel. I say "hotel" but it was more often some dodgy seaside B&B with mouldy walls and a bed like a park bench. You'd get a cuppa and a bit of soggy toast for your breakfast in the morning, and then you were off to play cricket for the next three days. One place in Brighton which will remain nameless had rats scampering around the dining room. It was like the Black Hole of Calcutta crossed with Fawlty Towers.'

'Were the accommodations always like that?' I asked.

'Not always,' Murray conceded. 'Some of them were worse. The grub was always a problem. You'd turn up at midnight somewhere like Blackpool or Cardiff and you'd be lucky to rustle up a few slices of sweaty pink meat with some congealed gravy. It still gives me the willies. The senior pro – it was old Jim Sims when I started – sometimes slipped the landlady a few extra quid just to make sure we got a hot meal at night. Let's just say most cricketers weren't exactly living in the lap of luxury back then. This was Middlesex, too, one of the posher counties, not that you would've known it from the pros' dressing-room: we had a thin strip of mud-coloured carpet on the floor, a lot of cracked lino, a few knackered chairs and some splintered wooden lockers for all the equipment; I bought most of Patsy Hendren's old gear for a fiver. And this was Lord's, remember. You can imagine what life was like somewhere like Glamorgan.'

Still, there were compensations.

'People loved to play at Old Trafford,' Murray reflected, growing wistful at the memory, 'and not just because of the ground facilities or the pleasure of having a go at Lancashire. Everyone got in cabs after stumps there and went down to the Mere Country Club. It was a big old Victorian pile out in Cheshire with a golf course and crested gates and ivy creeping up the walls. Very friendly place. Nice comfy rooms. It all happened there on a Saturday night, I can tell you. Funnily enough, the lads always wanted to play Lancashire away every year. I never saw Denis Compton happier than when he turned up for the first day's nets and saw that on the new season's fixture list.' Murray once asked me to help him find the *mot juste* to describe the state of most of his Middlesex team-mates, and county cricketers in general, when staying at the Mere, and 'merry' was the one we finally decided on, although 'totally legless' was another term that came to mind.

'After a while,' Murray continued, 'you got to know some of the better places to look in at on the county circuit. Another one was the old Red Lion [today's Danubius Hotel] right across the street from Lord's. Everyone nipped in there for a pint after stumps. No one bothered you unless Compo happened to walk in. The man was mobbed wherever he went. He was more popular than the pope or the PM in those days. Very genial, too – everyone was "old boy" to him – and still a class act, although as I say more likely to really turn it on in front of a full house at Lord's than he was for two men and a dog at Ilford.

For some reason he always took it up a notch against Yorkshire or Surrey. Loved a good challenge, too. I remember one of the lads, probably John Warr, winding Denis up one night at the Red Lion, telling him he was losing it and couldn't drive the ball straight anymore, and about the third or fourth delivery of the next morning's session came whistling back over the top for six and bloody nearly took Warr's head off on the dressing-room balcony while Denis waved his bat up at us. No one wound him up again after that.'

1957 clearly marked Murray's great leap forward as a professional cricketer, both as a wicketkeeper and a batsman. He not only did the double (the first time in 25 years this had happened) but scored his first championship century – 120 in the first innings of the away tie with Nottinghamshire, which was more than twice the total any of his Middlesex team-mates managed. Murray still spent his winters at home in west London, but his summers were a liberation. As he said, even in the dreariest venues 'I was still playing cricket every day and getting paid for it. I was young, and probably overdoing it a bit with the booze and birds. Life was good.'

At least part of this regimen was significantly modified one Sunday afternoon in the spring of 1958, when Murray happened to glance out of the window of his parents' home and see a strikingly attractive brunette sitting on the front wall of a house across the street. He had met her before, and went over to reacquaint himself. The young woman was called Colleen Bryan, and their wedding that September 'was the best thing that ever happened to me', Murray remarked nearly 60 years later. Their first child, Debbie, was born the next August.

'One of numerous reasons my marriage has lasted so long is that Colleen isn't sport minded,' Murray added. 'I knew she was pleased when I'd enjoyed a good day keeping or batting, but she never got carried away with anything like that. I'd come home after taking five catches or scoring a ton, and it would be "Well done, love, don't forget to take the rubbish out."' Colleen had an endearing, down-to-earth quality that won her many admirers whenever she did appear at Lord's or one of the other grounds. Tom Graveney once told me, 'I didn't pretend to know John well, but when you saw him and Colleen out together, bouncing stories and jokes off one another, laughing a lot, you knew that this was one of those marriages that last a lifetime.'

* * *

'My money is on Murray,' Bill Edrich wrote in his 1959 book *Round the Wicket*, when coming to assess England's immediate Test match prospects. Others had the same conviction. The selectors had named 24-year-old Brian Taylor of Essex as Godfrey Evans's deputy on the 1956/57 MCC tour of South Africa. Evans himself came to believe this particular choice 'a big mistake – Brian was a perfectly good county keeper who was out of his depth at that level. The general feeling was that he only got the nod in the first place because Doug Insole [England's vice-captain on the tour] knew him at Essex and thought he'd be a nice bloke to have around. He was, but you need something a bit more than that when you're away for six months playing cricket for your country.'

Twenty-five-year-old Roy Swetman of Surrey toured Australia with the MCC side in 1958/59, playing the first of his 11 Tests when Evans was injured. The shock loss of the Ashes that winter brought about one of those familiar bouts of wholesale reorganisation of English Test cricket. Evans lost his place after 13 years as the country's primary wicketkeeper, and promptly announced his retirement. For the next two years the selectors alternated between Swetman and Jim Parks of Sussex, the latter of whom effectively marks the start of the modern love affair with the batsman-wicketkeeper. Parks himself disarmingly told me that he never considered himself 'much more than a stopgap keeper ... I was really a specialist batsman for years, and it was only when Sussex were playing Essex one day and our stumper got hurt before the start that the skipper looked at me and said, "You're doing it." I didn't have a clue about wicketkeeping. I didn't have any kit, either, so I had to go in to the Essex dressing-room and borrow Brian Taylor's gloves.' The general feeling on the circuit was that Parks's keeping to the spinners was a hit-or-miss affair, but to his credit he proved extremely agile when standing back to the seamers. His popular nickname among his fellow professionals was 'the goalie'.

The end of Godfrey Evans's long reign as England's wicketkeeper presented certain opportunities, then, for an ambitious young player hoping to make the job his own. It bothered Evans that he was no longer the lightning-fast stumper who had dominated the Test scene for so long with a combination of technical prowess and vocally aggressive imposition on the opposing batsmen. Keith Miller once recalled, 'Trying to play your shots with Evans breathing down your neck was a sort of ordeal by fire. "How's your sister?" you'd hear as the likes of Alec Bedser thundered in at you. But more than that, Godders was obviously a brilliant technician – he had the reflexes for the really slick pick-up, the impossible catch or stumping, and he seemed to shoot out a telescopic arm to take the wayward delivery. He caught nicks no one else would have considered a chance.' Evans told me he saw himself when he looked at Murray, because, the sledging aside, both were keepers who liked to remind the man on strike that they were there, ready to pounce. Evans said: 'John was a lot smoother character than me. Less manic. I always bollocked the fielder if he screwed something up, Murray just rolled his eyes and got on with it. Don't panic, was his motto. But neither of us ever gave the batsman an inch.'

The sheer energy, manic or not, that Murray expended in this period was impressive: he played 32 first-class matches in the home 1960 season, which meant a total of 96 days' cricket packed in to just four months, quite apart from the demands of travel and cheap hotels, and the minor consideration of his home life. He was consistent, too. The scorecards show him regularly disposing of three or four batsmen a match, as often as not to the bowling of Fred Titmus. It's true his own batting fell off, although he was still capable of fireworks when the occasion demanded – the time he belted 68 in around half an hour against Leicestershire, for instance, after the new Middlesex captain John Warr had suggested they might get on with it, or when, with his team needing five runs to beat Hampshire at Lord's with nine wickets down, he pulled a Derek Shackleton bouncer into the grandstand for a towering six. He also represented the Players in that quintessentially English annual grudge match against the Gentlemen at Lord's, although the weather, grim and sunless at the start, eventually forced an early abandonment.

When all the figures were added up, Murray had brought off 95 catches and seven stumpings in first-class play. This was significantly more than any other English keeper. Although John himself never much cared for statistics, it's worth noting that compared to this haul of 102 dismissals Jim Parks, who represented England in all five Tests that summer, managed a total of just 74, while for Brian Taylor and Roy Swetman the figures fall to 59 and 55 respectively. All four men played the same amount of cricket.

Murray's reward came with his selection for a Test-level team raised by the MCC to tour New Zealand from December 1960 to March 1961. The itinerary included ten first-class matches, three of them against the national side. The tourists were led by 29-year-old Dennis Silk of Somerset, a man who appealed to the tradition of appointing amateur captains from the ancient universities, and there were also places in the squad for the likes of Bob Barber, Eric Russell, Roger Prideaux, Doug Padgett, Willie Watson and David Larter, Test players all. Murray avoided scoring many runs but was brilliant behind the stumps. Because we don't have his like today, it's hard to convey the boost to a fielding team's morale of a keeper who habitually stands up to even the medium-fast bowlers. Certainly no batsman could ever feel entirely comfortable with Murray poised immediately behind, waiting to dispatch him. Even a strokeplayer like John Reid, the holder of 58 New Zealand Test caps, who liked to come down the track because 'it puts the bowler off', broke his rule when he looked round and saw 'JT so close behind me that the peak of his cap shaded the bails.' Murray played eight matches and took 30 dismissals on the tour.

He recalled:

> 'I was playing pretty well by then. We had fun, too, although, again, you wouldn't recognise it compared to a modern England tour. There was no money, and most of us were billeted with local families. Plenty to eat and drink, though, and big civic banquets nearly every Friday and Saturday night. One or two of the lads used to get up and give unsolicited speeches, and I remember Willie [Watson] rising to his feet in a hotel dining room to spin tales, many of which he repeated, endlessly, over the course of a long evening. His audience didn't mind. They just wanted to mingle with famous English cricketers. Besides, they were drunk as well. I recall Dennis Silk appearing for breakfast one morning with the biggest black eye you ever saw, although I'm sure he just walked in to a door or something. As I say, all good fun.'

* * *

While John Murray was establishing himself as the de facto England Test wicketkeeper in New Zealand, I was a four-year-old child living on the other side of the world in Washington DC, where my father, by now a middle-ranking Royal Navy officer, happened to be on secondment in the planning echelons of NATO at the Pentagon. On 20 January 1961, a sunny but bitterly cold day, we had a modest berth in one of the stands to watch John F. Kennedy's inauguration as US president. Kennedy told the crowd that he was of that 'new generation of Americans – born in this century, tempered by war, disciplined by a hard and bitter peace, proud of our ancient heritage.' Later came the famous line about 'Ask not what your country can do for you, ask what you can do for your country' and its lesser-known sequel, 'Ask not what America will do for you, but what together we can do for the freedom of man.' My parents sometimes used to have muttered conversations about Kennedy's sex life, and the fact that two of his personal secretaries went by the names of Fiddle and Faddle. It was all a long way from cricket.

We were still in town six months later when the sock-puppet first secretary of East Germany's ruling Socialist Unity Party, Walter Ulbricht, decided to erect an 'anti-Fascist protection device' – or Berlin Wall, as others preferred to call it – although we were back living in the less racy world of suburban Guildford by the time the Cuban Missile Crisis erupted in October 1962. I had never consciously heard the name John Murray at that stage. My father wasn't one to dwell on the transience of human life, but I remember him being moved by the untimely death of the prolific sports writer and statistician Roy Webber, a sort of prototype Bill Frindall, in November 1962. He liked the fact that Webber had 'just told it straight', and he didn't care for most of the opinionated thought-pieces or confessional ghosted articles that came to typify cricket journalism later in that swinging decade.

* * *

On the Saturday morning of 3 June 1961, Middlesex began a three-day county championship match against Warwickshire at Lord's. Murray took his regulation three catches in the Warwickshire first innings. Back then no one played first-class cricket on a Sunday, so the next afternoon he was relaxing at home with his family when the five o'clock news came on the radio, and after a bit about the latest sterling crisis and the spy George Blake getting 42 years for espionage, the announcer said in his most sombre tones, as if introducing coverage of a state funeral, that they were going over to Lord's to hear the names of the England team chosen to play Australia in the summer's first Test at Edgbaston beginning on Thursday. Murray was the wicketkeeper. Having gone from first picking up a bat to playing for Middlesex in just five years, it had taken him nearly another decade to step up to international level.

'The radio announcement was the first I'd heard of it,' he remembered. 'On the Monday a letter came telling me to report to Birmingham, second-class return, on Wednesday. I was only sorry my Dad didn't live to see it. I was excited, obviously, but on the other hand it's just another of the gradual rungs up the ladder, from the seconds to the county side and then on to touring with MCC. Oddly enough, a big part of the thrill was getting an England blazer. I remember walking around in it on the morning of the Test and feeling like a million quid. It's important to look good when you're playing at that level, and years later I was talking to Richie Benaud about how you never wanted to let your opponent see you slouching around in jeans or trainers. Any sign of weakness was the quickest way for them to size you up and take advantage. It was all about perception. Richie was amused. He'd always operated on the same principle.'

In the end Murray went up to Birmingham not by train but as a passenger in the England captain Colin Cowdrey's silver Mark VII Jaguar. Cowdrey had been passing through London and genially offered the new boy a lift. 'I was a bit nervous by then, but when I got in the car Colin said simply, "Congratulations, JT." It was perfect because it was so ordinary.' Murray always respected Cowdrey, but 'it was an odd sort of drive up. Every ten miles or so he'd pull off the main road and turn down some country lane where he'd stop at somebody's bloody great manor house, say "Won't be a minute", and I'd sit there in the driveway while Colin went in to see whoever it was. Then he used to pull out these sheets of paper from the glove compartment and show them to me when we stopped at red lights. Basically they were diagrams of the Edgbaston playing area and Cowdrey would say things like, "If Trueman bowls to Lawry from the pavilion end, do we want to start off with a leg gully, or a man closer to backward square leg?" Well, what the hell do I know? Colin was a bit like that, always sweating the fine detail. Lovely bloke, brilliant batsman, but no self-confidence. Didn't have the killer instinct. This went on all afternoon, until we finally pulled up at the team hotel in Droitwich. I got out and started hauling my kit from the back seat of the Jag. There might still be time for a swift net before dinner, I thought. Just then Gubby Allen, the chairman of selectors, came trotting down the front steps wearing a beautiful pinstripe suit with a carnation in the buttonhole and offered us both a glass of sherry.'

# 3.

# BRIGHTER CRICKET

'GOING out to bat, I felt terrible,' Murray recalled of his experience during the final session of his first day of Test cricket at Edgbaston. 'Cowdrey had won the toss and for some reason decided to go in on a green wicket. It rained on and off all afternoon. Right after tea Mike Smith was out for a duck off the last ball of a Slasher Mackay over. I was sitting on a hard seat behind the dressing-room window, trying to get mentally ready. The way things were going, I thought I might have another half an hour or so to wait.

'The first ball of Slasher's next over was an outswinger that Subba Row steered straight to Bobby Simpson at slip, who caught it. Fred Trueman poked his head round from the balcony and shouted, "You're on, sunshine." That was it. There was some red-faced old buffer in a blazer standing by the door downstairs, and as I passed by him he said, "Don't worry, John. You won't be

Both stories involved former English Test batting greats. The first came on the second day of the match when Denis Compton appeared in the home dressing-room and told Murray: 'I'm on the telly at 3pm, and I want you to swing your arms around and jump up and down exactly then so that I can talk about you on the air,' which may help to explain the puzzling sight of England's famously suave and unflappable wicketkeeper suddenly going into a paroxysm that looked like a frenzied native fertility dance in between deliveries.

The other encounter came shortly after Murray was out, c Davidson, b Benaud, on the first evening. 'The door of the dressing-room opened, and in came Sir Len Hutton, no less. He walked over and planted himself on a hard chair in front of me. After that there was complete silence for about a minute. Eventually Hutton pulled a packet of fags out of his pocket and lit one up. After a couple of puffs he cleared his throat, looked me up and down, and finally said: "Was it the flipper, John?" I said that yes, Benaud had bowled me a top-spinner and it was on me before I was properly in position for the stroke. Hutton nodded, then took a few more leisurely drags of his cigarette. Since he apparently wasn't going to say anything further on the subject, I got up the nerve to ask him how I should have played that particular shot. Certain other men might have responded with reams of technical stuff about the correct position of the feet and the exact angle of the bat at the point of contact, and all that. Len's only reply was: "If you don't hit it in the air, they can't catch it."'

* * *

Australia won the low-scoring second Test at Lord's, despite Trueman's six wickets and Murray's four catches in the match. The *Telegraph* report referred to the 'sharp' England wicketkeeping. Trueman was on form again in the next Test, on his native heath at Leeds, with a match return of 11-88; England won by eight wickets. When it came to Old Trafford, however, Murray remembered a distressing incident when Peter May, who was back as captain, threw the ball to Trueman after lunch on the fourth day and Trueman promptly threw it back again with the observation: 'Piss off, skipper. Let Closey bowl. I'm fucking knackered.' Murray thought May 'perhaps too accommodating to Fred' in the matter, and, not privy to the on-field debate, Ron Roberts wrote of the subsequent passage of play:

> 'May tossed the ball to Brian Close ... He is apt to need a couple of overs to strike a length, and this was an inopportune time to introduce a bowler of erratic tendencies. O'Neill soon took three fours off him.'

Close returned figures of 0-33, and Australia won the Test by 54 runs after May was famously bowled behind his legs for a second-innings duck. The result meant that Australia would retain the Ashes, although there was at least some consolation for the home team during their six-night residency at the nearby Mere Country Club, particularly for those players who took a more relaxed view of their wedding vows than Murray himself did. The fifth and final Test at the Oval was drawn. Rain washed out more than half the fourth day. Murray finished the series with 18 dismissals, then an English wicketkeeping record against Australia, and a batting average of 20, which happened to be exactly the same target with the bat Cowdrey had set for him when they first set out together up the A40 to Droitwich. He took away a cheque 'in the hundreds rather than thousands' for his summer's work.

* * *

Once Murray finished with the Australians he had time to play in Middlesex's final three championship matches, passing 1,000 first-class runs for the season as he did so, before flying off with an MCC team under Ted Dexter's captaincy for a four-month tour of India and Pakistan. It was a mixed success. Dexter told me: 'John was a great man to have on tour in that part of the world, where things can become pretty ropy (dodgy transport, accommodation, food, etc). He was the one to smile most in adversity and to keep up the spirits of those less able to see the bright side.' In this same context, Ken Barrington long remembered the 'stomach-turning' scenes in the dining room of one of the side's hotels in rural India, where, assessing the situation, Murray 'marched in to the kitchen, evicting about an Aussie-rules team's worth of rats there, and emerged again half an hour later, triumphantly carrying these huge pots piled high with delicious English grub: Cottage pie, steak and kidney, eggs, chips, beans, the lot. We could have been back home in Surrey.' It wasn't the last time Murray would be glad of his experience in the cookery school at RAF Innsworth. He spent Christmas Day of 1961 in the eastern Indian city of Cuttack, about 6,000 miles from home. England lost the Test series with India 2-0, but won against Pakistan 1-0. After that, they would not win another series in Pakistan for 39 years.

Murray's deputy on the subcontinent was the 27-year-old Nottinghamshire wicketkeeper-batsman Geoff Millman. Millman, previously off the selectors' (and most other people's) radar, was one of those perfectly competent but slightly anonymous characters so prevalent in the English county championship. His county team-mate 'Bomber' Wells once described him to me: 'A decent bloke, and a capable if not scintillating cricketer. At best an adequate stumper, at worst an embarrassing one. The impression he left was of not leaving an impression.' Nonetheless, Millman had scored 1,350 first-class runs in 1961, and had once taken five catches in an innings against Essex at Westcliff while Wells himself, better known as an off-spinner, had swatted 39 in a couple of overs off the bowling of England's Barry Knight and Trevor Bailey. His colleagues did not name him Bomber for nothing.

By the time England came to play India in the third Test at Delhi in December 1961, Murray was possibly not on peak form. Few of the tourists were. The home team amassed 466 in nearly two days, and after an equally leisurely-paced century by Barrington – an innings of 'monk-like meditation', one critic wrote – the game was always behind the clock. A draw was inevitable long before a thunderstorm flooded the ground on the final day. Murray himself took no catches and didn't bat. Everything in that Test seemed to happen in slow motion. 'It was like playing cricket underwater,' Murray recalled. The next morning, some of the tourists set out in what Peter Parfitt calls a plane 'of Wright Brothers vintage' for a stormy 300-mile flight upcountry to a match in Jullundar, 'and some of us weren't happy about it. Most of the boys on the plane weren't even playing in that particular game, and there was a lot of grumbling about what we were doing being bounced around in the sky somewhere over northern India when we could just as well have been safe and sound back at the hotel. This went on for a while, until John, who had been sitting there silently up until then, leant forward, tapped the pilot on the shoulder and politely said, "Please turn around and take us back to Delhi." And he did.'

Ted Dexter added that 'Murray's loyalty to me was beyond question, and his quiet but determined disposition was a perfect balance for some of the more capricious or occasionally explosive characters on the tour.' One of the wicketkeeper's daily maxims was: 'Never hurry – either on the field or off it.' That policy would have put him as one with the glacial tempo of the Delhi Test, and with most of the cricket on the tour as a whole. But Murray took at least some of the fall for the collective torpor, and when the two teams met again at Calcutta, Millman – 'largely because of his expert batting', the anonymous *Times* correspondent thought – made his Test debut behind the stumps. India won the match by 187 runs. Millman scored nought in the first innings and four in the second. He was still in the team for the fifth and final Test at Madras. India won again, although this time Millman managed 32 and 14. *Wisden* praised him for his 'quiet efficiency'. At that stage Murray flew home for his varicose veins operation ('Some people inherit money, I got bad legs,' he liked to say), which lost him his tour bonus as a result, and left Millman, now supported by Jimmy Binks of Yorkshire, in possession for the rest of the tour and the first two Tests against Pakistan in the 1962 home season.

Cricket is a cruel game, but over the years Murray probably came to know its twin triumphs and disasters better than most. He'd waited nine years to break in to the England team, and now he was out again – sacrificed for what a critic called the 'clearly superior' all-round skills of an older rival who finished the Pakistan tour with a Test batting average of three. You had to laugh, and in fact Murray did so. He sometimes told me the story of one of the numerous letters he received after coming home early from India in January 1962. While there were many congratulatory or sympathetic notes, the one that best captured the true spirit of professional sport (even cricket) came from a former England captain of notably unsentimental outlook on life. 'Dear John,' the letter read, 'Hard shit.' In time Murray returned to a Test-strength MCC team to play Surrey at Lord's. In figures alone, the match rated as a successful comeback. Surrey lost only six batsmen in both innings combined. Murray caught three of them, and 'would have had a fourth if the umpire had been awake'.

Here's what *Wisden* had to say in its only mixed review of his work that season:

> 'Murray greatly fell away with the bat, but his wicket-keeping remained good and he eventually won back his place in the England side.'

The cold statistics are that in 20 first-class matches that wet summer, Murray scored just 362 runs at an average of 20, and that he accounted for 46 catches and six stumpings. Of course there were exceptions to this comparatively ordinary record. No matter how grim his batting at any given moment, Murray remained capable of the glittering cameo knock of 40 or 50, just as he did of the swift dismissal brought about with the air of ease and simplicity that characterised his overall game. At his best he regularly took catches – hard and low or hard and high – somewhere in the V between about third slip and leg gully, and there was a dramatic moment in the match between Middlesex and Worcestershire at Lord's in mid-May when the visitors' left-handed Dick Richardson played a genuine leg-glance off the lively medium pace of Ron Hooker and Murray, standing up to the stumps, shot out his right hand, caught the ball, calmly flipped it back to his friend Peter Parfitt at slip and then stood there fiddling around with his cap and gloves for a bit, all during the time it took the batsman to process the fact that he was out. Tom Graveney was at the other end and remembered, 'It was one of those "Godfrey Evans" moments when you blink and say to yourself, "What just happened?"'

Like Graveney himself, Murray eventually clawed his way back in to the Test team that summer. In their own ways they were probably the two great stylists of English cricket, and it seemed to more than a few of England's gleeful opponents over the years that some sort of mistake had been made whenever either of them was allowed to slip out of the side. Garry Sobers once told me that the West Indian tourists had 'literally punched the air' when listening to the news on their hotel radio announcing that Graveney and Murray had again been overlooked for a home Test in 1963, and that 'a couple of nice guys but total nonentities at that level' had replaced them.

Relieving Millman of his place behind the stumps in the third Test of the 1962 series at Headingley, Murray 'did everything right', *The Times* reported, and England won by an innings. He took five catches in the next Test, a draw at Trent Bridge, and another handful of them at the Oval, where curiously enough he opened the England second innings when they went out needing to score 27 to win on the fourth afternoon. The *Daily Telegraph* said of the series: 'Murray was restrained with the bat, but did sharp work in the field.' Tom Graveney finished his own season with a Test batting average of 100.25.

* * *

Although English cricket in 1961/62 wasn't the fluorescent-clad jamboree it later became, a mild sense of adventure could be glimpsed in such developments as the appointment of the raffish Ted Dexter as the nation's Test captain and that of the former Middlesex skipper Walter Robins (like Dexter, the maverick all-rounder of his day) as chairman of selectors. Robins promptly began his tenure by issuing an ultimatum to first-class cricketers. *Wisden* summarised this as 'Play aggressively at all times; otherwise you will not be chosen for England.'

The results, taken as a whole, were predictably mixed, although Murray remembered 'a few more batsmen probably came out of their creases, and there was a bit better fielding around'. 'It cannot be said that Robins's policy produced precisely the effects desired,' *Wisden* was forced to admit, after England had lost two of their next four series and drawn the rest, 'but at least it relieved cricket of some of the stagnation which threatened its popularity at the time.' Attendances for championship matches had fallen from a total of 2.2 million cash-paying customers in 1947 to just over 700,000 in 1962. As

Murray remarked, 'Frankly, the only way I could ever afford to spend eight hours a day at a county cricket match was by actually playing in it. You looked around at some of those grounds when you went out to bat on a damp Tuesday morning at Rushden and it was so quiet you could hear people in the stands talking to each other. About halfway out to the middle one day I sneezed, and a bloke sitting by himself behind the square leg boundary looked up and said "Bless you".'

It was a salutary assessment of cricket's financial prospects, then, rather than some hazy concession to the newly 'swinging' times that led to the (it seemed to traditionalists) impossibly tasteless introduction of limited-overs tournaments such as the Gillette Cup. Under Dexter's astute captaincy Sussex won the first two annual trophies. The concept as a whole was an immediate success with the public. Reviewing the first Gillette Cup final in September 1963, the veteran sports writer Peter Wilson enthused that 'Lord's, the temple of tradition, could be transformed into a reasonable replica of Wembley ... a sell-out with rosettes, singing, cheers, jeers and counter-cheers. This triumphant sporting experiment ... may not have been cricket to the purists, but by golly it was just the stuff the doctor ordered.'

An even more seismic shift in the game's established order had come in November 1962, when the MCC accepted the verdict of its advisory committee (reached only by ten votes to seven) to abolish the distinction between the amateur gentleman and the professional player. From then on, they would all be known simply by the egalitarian term 'cricketers'. Dissolving the social formula that had stood at the heart of the domestic game for over 150 years was not a universally welcomed move. Just four years earlier, a similar committee had conducted an inquiry and decided against what it termed the 'incautious step' of fundamentally changing the status of English cricket. Writing in the decidedly non-radical *Daily Telegraph*, E.W. Swanton deplored the loss of the independent player, and reminded his readers that 'the evolution of the game has been stimulated from its beginnings by the fusion of the two strains, each of which [has] drawn strength and inspiration from the other. Cricket has been at its best when there has been an even balance.'

By the mid-1960s, Middlesex's capped players, among them the championship's elite, could each expect to earn between £800 and £900 a season, depending on results. An England Test cricketer got £110 a match, and £700–800 for a winter tour. A true superstar like Yorkshire's Fred Trueman (notwithstanding his unfortunate habit of routinely forfeiting his £50 'good conduct' bonus) probably took home £3,500 a year, which was about three times the going rate for a provincial shop assistant, but still only on a par with a junior civil servant or a mid-ranking London bank officer.

Murray was at heart a socially conservative, or old-school, character, and as such he viewed some of the innovations of early 1960s cricket as 'dubious but probably necessary ways of putting more bums on seats'. The Middlesex dressing-room of the time was quite evenly divided between the hardened professional and the paternalistic amateur. 'John was highly unusual because he had a foot in both camps,' Fred Titmus told me. 'He was obviously outside of the magic circle of public school men, but he had a bluff, common-sense approach they respected. It was quite rare in those days. The officer class and the Other Ranks both looked up to him.'

Mike Brearley added:

> 'John had strong views about the spirit in which the game should be played ... He believed that standards of play declined overall during his career, and connected this with the lessening of discipline in cricket and life in general. At the same time, he was always aware of the limited rights a cricketer had in the face of arbitrary, whimsical or uninformed decisions by administrators, and of the limited say players had in the running of the game.'

A moderate and eminently practical shop steward, Murray never hesitated to rally round any fellow pro in need of advice or support, and in 1967 was one of those responsible for the launching of the Cricketers' Association, for many years serving as its treasurer.

* * *

It was in this somewhat febrile social atmosphere that the selectors met at Lord's in July 1962 to determine the best candidate to lead that winter's MCC tour to Australia. Dexter was the man in possession, but found a rival in his own former Sussex captain, 33-year-old Reverend David Sheppard, who was willing to take a sabbatical from his church mission in the east end of London. Sheppard had returned to county cricket after a two-year absence only in June 1962. He scored 108 in his first innings. It was a sensational comeback, and the press began to agitate for his England appointment. Sheppard was hailed as 'a fine leader on and off the field' and photographed (in clerical garb) jumping gleefully over a brick wall. A month later, he opened the Gentlemen's batting in what proved to be the last ever Gents v Players match at Lord's. This time he scored 112. That evening's headlines were all variants of 'Good Sheppard' and the like, and beneath them came many a story extolling the drama and romance of the whole experiment. Next morning, Dexter was named captain.

Not untypical was the reaction of the *Daily Mirror*: 'Good Lord, It's Ted.' The press had another shock when the tour manager was revealed as the sixteenth Duke of Norfolk, Earl Marshal of England, with Alec Bedser in support. An unqualified admirer of Dexter the player, Murray privately had his doubts about his captain's man-management skills when subjected to the protracted strain of a six-month Ashes tour. He was right to do so. 'There were moments when you'd look round in the heat of a Test at Sydney, and there was Ted practising his golf swing at square leg rather than encouraging the bowler or moving the field.' Dexter's fondness for horse racing exceeded even that for golf. He carried a portable television around to watch the action from Epsom or Ascot, and once declared a Sussex innings from Brighton Racecourse. The spirit of Dexter's core philosophy of his career was probably best captured when he later wrote: 'I got into [cricket] by finding I could do it successfully at a certain level and wanting to know whether I could do it at the highest level. Once I discovered I could, the game became a great turn-on. Then I began to wonder what I was doing in it.'

In the same vein, Murray thought the MCC tour manager 'a lovely old boy, very kind to me, but not someone you'd normally see getting the team bus lined up, or helping to carry everyone's gear in and out of hotels. All the really hard graft was on Big Al's shoulders.' Murray's own notional deputy in Australia was the 26-year-old sometime Oxford University and Warwickshire wicketkeeper Alan 'A.C.' Smith, who, in a familiar tale, batted better on tour and in the end played in most of the Tests.

* * *

On 25 September 1962, Murray, having kissed his family goodbye for the next six months, spent the evening at 'some sort of one-star brick hotel' on the fringes of Heathrow airport before flying out early the next morning with the MCC party to Aden. Only 16 of the 17 players actually boarded the flight, because 32-year-old Brian Statham made his own travel arrangements. The veteran England seamer had previously expressed his misgivings both about having to leave his sickly wife at home in Lancashire and the tour in general, and so obtained permission to make his own way to Australia by the shortest means possible. Fred Trueman was 'not chuffed' at this special treatment of his opening-bowling partner, Murray recalled.

That was nothing compared to Trueman's wrath during the team's subsequent 11-day voyage from Aden to Freemantle on board the SS *Canberra*, where Dexter discovered the former Olympic athlete Gordon Pirie was a fellow passenger. Pirie was invited to organise a series of pre-breakfast training sessions for the cricketers. The idea was to circumnavigate the deck for the equivalent of a three-mile run, a not wholly welcome initiative to tourists who had just endured a long domestic season, and things got 'a little tense', in Murray's nuanced phrase, as a result. Pirie himself was soon in splendid isolation. Certain players found that it was possible to duck down a nearby corridor, have a smoke, and then emerge later to rejoin the field as it approached the finish line. (Trueman took the more robust approach of threatening to throw Pirie overboard.) When the *Canberra* docked on 9 October, *The Times* correspondent unblushingly told his readers, 'There will never be a fitter English cricket side than that arriving today.' Pirie himself demurred in his own published article, in which he remarked that the players were 'lazy, decrepit, bolshie and insubordinate'. Trueman then went on to admit in the *Sydney Morning Herald* to wondering if the Tests would be played under Jockey Club rules – a reference to his manager's and captain's mutual fondness for the turf – or be held in a Church Mission, perhaps alluding to David Sheppard's presence on the tour. The Yorkshire legend, who later expressed reservations about the arrival of Dexter's wife Susan on a modelling assignment, would as usual be docked his £50 good conduct bonus at the end of the visit.

The cricket itself got underway with a two-day match against Western Australia Country at Kalgoorlie, about 400 miles inland of Perth. Murray didn't bat in the first innings and top-scored with 102, including two sixes and 15 fours, in the second. He had no way of knowing that this early success would probably constitute the high point of his tour. Three weeks later, the Cuban Missile Crisis having intervened, he was keeping in an upcountry game at Griffith, somewhere west of Sydney (in the electoral seat of Murray), when the part-time spinner Geoff Pullar bowled a rank long-hop to the home team's Ken McMullen. McMullen, an Australian rugby union international who was then learning to play a reasonable grade of cricket as a summer alternative, caught the wicketkeeper with the flat of his bat as he smashed the ball to the boundary. Murray was helped from the field covered in blood and needed six stitches in his forehead, which were inserted by an elderly local physio in a back room of the pavilion. There was some talk about a possible broken jaw. Back in the family's new home in north Wembley, Colleen Murray picked up her party-line phone early one icy morning and was surprised to hear the Duke of Norfolk at the other end, assuring her that whatever she might have read in the press to the contrary her husband was all right. Oddly enough, that was the first she had heard of the matter. Murray's jaw was found to be intact, but he missed the next two matches, and when the side for the first Test at Brisbane was announced Smith was preferred behind the stumps. A perfectly efficient stopper, he took three catches and put a couple of others down in the course of the match, which was drawn.

Murray wasn't bitter. He enjoyed the tour, which in time came to assume some of the qualities of a paid holiday for him. It's worth repeating that he 'endlessly admired' Dexter as a player, and more particularly as a batsman whose mission statement was to 'turn the tables on the bowler as quickly as possible', a credo illustrated by several murderously potent innings in Australia. But the dashing England skipper was not, one has to say, the sort of leader content just to follow the manual with little or no variation, and this absolute refusal to accept handed-down truths – whether as a player or, later, administrator – remained the one constant factor in Dexter's character. He was, and is, an energetic, imaginative, romantic sort with a low tolerance for the mundane details of life. The mantle of leadership which fell to him on Peter May's retirement did not always rest comfortably on his shoulders.

In Australia, Dexter felt free, perhaps obliged, to indulge his many theories, which ran the gamut from his preference for a 'really sound wicketkeeper-batsman [over] a sometime genius specialist player', as he put it to a senior colleague, up to the Ashes themselves, which he deemed 'a bane and a nuisance … they should be abolished and each man paid £1,000 for a result'. Tom Graveney once told me that he, too, had keenly respected Dexter's technical prowess with the bat, but that 'he was one of those blokes who can't drink a cup of tea without having a strategy for it. In my humble opinion, Murray didn't put a foot wrong on that tour. His only sin was to have a captain who was temperamentally a bit flaky, and who actually thought that Alan Smith, a very decent county player in his way, was anywhere near good enough to be the England wicketkeeper.'

The tourists ate their Christmas lunch that year in the grand hall of the South Australian Hotel in Adelaide, where as many as 200 cricketers, officials and travelling reporters concluded the meal with a lusty if off-key rendition of 'Waltzing Matilda'. England's four amateur players had earlier made speeches of varying lengths, while the other 13 men weren't called upon. Later in the afternoon everyone went out for a golf match and sweep at the nearby Royal Adelaide club. Fifty-four-year-old Don Bradman won the day, and not surprisingly, Murray recalled, 'as he was the only one there who was sober'. Six weeks later, Bradman agreed to briefly come out of retirement to captain a Prime Minister's XI against MCC at Canberra. He had not played a first-class innings for 14 years and he scored just four before playing an innocuous ball from Statham which somehow trickled down from the inside edge on to his pads and brushed the wicket, dislodging a bail. The tourists immediately rushed up in an animated posse to surround the umpire, muttering variants of 'Call an effing no-ball', but Bradman had already walked off – 'Like 1948 at the Oval all over again,' Murray remarked.

England won the second Test at Melbourne, largely thanks to the batting of Dexter, Sheppard and Cowdrey, although their fellow amateur Smith scored just six in over an hour at the crease and seemed to one critic to be 'not necessarily out of his depth, but slightly uninspiring, as an admiralty civil servant might appear in a room full of pirates'. The author Alan Ross wrote of a moment in the Australian first innings when a ball from Statham found the edge of Lawry's bat, 'but Smith was rootedly slow in getting across and the ball shot for four'. Ross added: 'The [other] available wicketkeeper would have swallowed it.' Perhaps that was Dexter's own feeling on the matter, because Murray was back in the side for the third Test at Sydney. There was a crowd of 55,000 on hand to see him be given out lbw – after some deliberation – for nought on the first day. Next morning he took a horizontal catch ('diving at least 12 feet to do so', Peter Parfitt remembered) to dismiss Lawry off Worcestershire's Len Coldwell, dislocating his shoulder as he thudded to earth. Parfitt himself had to take over behind the stumps, although a heavily medicated Murray batted again in the rearguard second innings – managing an unbeaten three in 100 minutes as the Australians put seven men around him, their hands outstretched as if expecting him to swoon at any moment, but, conversely, never once bowling him a bouncer. 'They'd never be so chivalrous today,' he smiled 40 years later. Richie Benaud told me he thought Murray 'the best technical keeper in the world at this stage, [someone] you never noticed until he did something really brilliant', as well as a 'smashing guy' to boot, and that under the circumstances 'none of our team would have cared to see him further hurt'. Australia won that match by eight wickets. Smith came back for the fourth and fifth Tests, both of which were drawn.

It had all been a somewhat fractious series off the field, even if Crawford White perhaps overstated the case when informing his readers in the *Daily Express* with the crisp, simple authority that was the hallmark of his long years of cricket reporting:

> 'All Australia is seething with savage, indignant reaction to the ghastly flop of the MCC tour. And if Ted Dexter survives the broadsides to captain England against West Indies this summer he will be a very lucky man.'

In fact Dexter did survive, but before that there was also a brief but hectic tour of New Zealand to negotiate. There was another small demonstration of the England captain's distinctive and sometimes mildly whimsical approach to his job shortly after the team's arrival at their Auckland hotel late on the evening of 22 February 1963. Dexter called Murray and Smith in to his room and told them, 'We'll play one of you for the first Test and the other one for the second Test, and we'll see how it goes for the third.' As a result, Murray walked on to the field at Eden Park the next morning knowing that he had already been dropped from the side that would play New Zealand a few days later at Wellington. 'Not the most brilliant case of man-management,' he remarked drily. Murray didn't know that the Auckland Test would in fact mark his last international appearance for two years.

When I once asked him to sum up his experience during the winter of 1962/63, Murray pursed his lips for a moment and then said that in retrospect he had fond memories of the whole thing and that three particular events, none of them happening on the field of play, stood out. They each reflect his eye for the small but telling detail.

The first came towards the end of the Australian leg of the tour, when someone had spotted the great if somewhat truculent Surrey left-armer Tony Lock on the ground. Much to everyone's surprise, not least his own, Lock had been left out of the MCC squad, but had then signed up to spend a highly successful winter playing for Western Australia. According to Murray, 'When Dexter saw him he flipped Lock the ball and gaily invited him to come bowl at us in the nets, and Lockie flung it straight back at Ted like a ruddy Exocet. It nearly took his head off.'

The second memory was when everyone had gathered for an outdoor group photograph after stumps one warm evening, and Murray's friend Ken Barrington (who finished the Test series with a batting average of 73) had duly appeared 'all spruced up in a beautiful new blazer, creased flannels and shiny white boots, every detail in order', only to then take a step backwards at the photographer's request and fall headlong into the ornamental koi pond he'd failed to notice behind him. 'I don't know whether it was because you get a bit silly when you're living away from home like that for six months, or if it's just what you're like when you're in your twenties, but I remember everyone fell about laughing. Kenny did, too. He always swore he found a goldfish in his jockstrap later that night.'

The third indelible memory Murray had was of the moment when the England team had walked in to the pavilion before the start of the first Test at Auckland, 'and some guy in a sort of traffic policeman's rig with a blue jacket and long white gloves promptly directed the three amateurs to a lounge upstairs and told the rest of us to keep going down until we ended up in a sort of cubbyhole in the basement that smelt of old fags and cat pee. Not that I'm complaining, but let's just say the whole social revolution in cricket took a bit longer to reach some parts than others.'

* * *

Incongruously dressed in their matching Burton's tropical suits, with a smattering of sunglasses here and there, the members of the MCC touring party arrived back in London in the freezing pre-dawn hours of 22 March 1963. It was the first any of the professional players had seen of their wives or loved ones for the past 179 days. Later that Friday morning, the balding but puckish figure of 48-year-old John Profumo, the Macmillan government's secretary of state for war, rose to his feet in the House of Commons to indignantly deny 'that there was any impropriety whatsoever in my acquaintanceship with Miss Christine Keeler'.

In fact, this was not an entirely accurate record of events. Twenty months earlier, on Saturday, 8 July 1961, Profumo had attended a party given by a society osteopath and sexual procurer named Stephen Ward at the country estate where he rented a summer cottage. At some point, they had walked out to the swimming pool and there encountered the 19-year-old Keeler, a striking brunette with stage ambitions, and her equally free-spirited blonde friend Mandy Rice-Davies, 17, a dancer and showgirl. Both young women were, as the jargon of the day had it, of doubtful reputation. Keeler, who emerged nude from the pool to demurely shake Profumo's hand, then happened to be in a relationship with Yevgeni Ivanov, the deputy Soviet naval attaché to Britain, and reportedly a confidant of the highest members of the Moscow politburo. Somehow inevitably, Keeler had then begun an affair with Profumo, which meant that she was sleeping both with the British war minister and an alleged Russian spy, thus bringing a national security dimension to the proceedings.

Two months after his rousing statement in parliament, Profumo (who was married to the film star Valerie Hobson) suddenly remembered that perhaps he had slept with Keeler after all, and that he was resigning his ministerial portfolio with immediate effect. He got a 'Dear Profumo' letter back from Macmillan, accepting his decision with alacrity. There were several further twists and turns to the whole protracted saga – eventually leading *The Times* to sigh, 'The entire United Kingdom Government has become a sort of brothel' – that lie outside the scope of a book about a cricket wicketkeeper, but taken as a whole it's widely agreed to have marked the ignition point to Britain's 1960s modernisation crisis. After Profumo, social deference was never quite the same again. Since John Kennedy delivered his iconic 'Ich bin ein Berliner' speech, the young Lennon and McCartney sat down in a Newcastle hotel room to write 'She Loves You' – the best-selling single of the Beatles' career, and the song that thrust them full-tilt into the spotlight – and the reforming Paul VI began his long reign as pope all at that same time, it's arguable that what we now call 'the Sixties' really began in the third week of June 1963. Rash as it generally is to try and assemble random historical facts into a neatly unified pattern that few people would have recognised as such at the time, with hindsight perhaps we can say that the simultaneous abolition of England's 'gentleman' and 'player' divide and the arrival of domestic knockout cricket with the Gillette Cup – the first match was played early that May at Old Trafford, and lasted two days because of rain – was broadly consistent with the other landmark changes taking place in society.

I once asked Murray about this seismic transformative shift occurring in English life, and he said: 'As far as I'm concerned, there wasn't a lot of difference between the game of cricket in 1962 and 1963, although I do remember Titmus once turning up in the Lord's pavilion wearing a sort of safari suit instead of a blazer and tie. *That* was new.'

* * *

Although Murray was chosen that May to represent the MCC against the touring West Indies at Lord's, usually a good sign of the selectors' intentions for the coming series, he again slipped out of the England team that season. For some compelling reason, Keith Andrew of Northants played in the first Test, nine years after his last one, and after that Ted Dexter's county colleague Jim Parks was again given the job seemingly because of his superior batting skills. It was a curious choice in the specific circumstances of 1963, because while Parks was always happiest against spin bowling the tourists' attack that summer tends to be remembered for the raw hostility of its pacemen Wes Hall and Charlie Griffith. At all events, England lost the series 3-1. In his four Tests, Parks scored a total of 190 runs at an average of 23. These were perfectly respectable figures (even Barrington managed a series average of just 27.50), if not exactly evidence of the long-handle technique Parks so thrillingly employed at the county and knockout level. Barrington himself told me in 1980:

> 'Jim was a very good player, always neat against spin, a go-getter, loved the one-day bash. [Murray] was a bit more of the old-fashioned school. He was better at the long haul, when the fight was hardest, when you had to go in before tea and hold an end up until the close. He could play his strokes, too. Figures don't really tell you about the full-blooded driving, or the hooking of the short ones right in front of his face – and he didn't need a helmet to help him do it.'

Alluding to this same textbook batting technique, a former Middlesex player with a later professional interest in the cinema added:

> 'I always thought JT was slumming it a bit in one-day cricket. You looked at him going out to the middle, beautifully trim, twirling his bat, could have been the first day of a Test match, and needing to whack about 80 in ten overs. It was like watching Laurence Olivier having to ham it up in a kung-fu movie.'

Murray's first contact with the 65-over Gillette Cup format seemed to confirm this view. Playing for Middlesex against Gloucestershire at Bristol on 22 May 1963, he went in with the score on 125/7 with orders to have a go, and was clean bowled for nought. Middlesex somehow won that game, but went out in the next round to Northants, for whom a burly young schoolteacher-cricketer named Colin Milburn blasted his way to an unorthodox 84. Milburn was 'not a business player', *The Times* wrote. Murray had another crack at the West Indies when they came back to Lord's to play Middlesex in late July. He scored 56 in the first innings and nine in the second innings, unbeaten both times, batting against a barrage of yorkers, throat balls and other deliveries that seemed to the watching *Daily Mail* correspondent to be 'of suspect legality', or, to put it another way, thrown. When the reigning county champions Yorkshire appeared at Lord's on a miserably wet Saturday morning in August Murray took five catches in the only fully completed innings of the match, though finding time later to hit Fred Trueman back over the top first bounce into the pavilion. Trueman himself greeted the shot by clapping his hands together above his head and then gesturing in the direction of the downstairs committee room. He later told Murray that he'd been trying to alert the 'old buggers' there to the actual spectacle of the cricket. 'But they just spend their time guzzling pink gins.'

The following week at Worcester, Murray took three more catches and a couple of stumpings while top-scoring with 59 out of a total of 234 against Ron Headley and Norman Gifford at their craftiest. Only one other Middlesex batsman passed 30. Murray played that day with a style and composure that impressed even Tom Graveney. 'John's batting was very much like his personality – correct, unpretentious, never wanting to hog the limelight. And that was just the second part of his game, remember. I saw a lot of good wicketkeepers at close quarters, and for about ten years John was simply the best there was.' Nonetheless, it was a mixed season for Murray, first losing his place in the Test side and then seeing Middlesex finish a modest sixth in the county table.

After the 1963 home series, the MCC, or England, sent a team on a seven-week, five-Test tour of India. Jim Parks and Jimmy Binks of Yorkshire were the keepers chosen ahead of a surprised and, for once, 'mildly cheesed off' Murray. Fred Titmus, who did go, later remarked: 'It hadn't been a great year for JT, and I don't think he felt particularly chuffed about the prospect of two months' hard graft in India.' Yet almost a half-century later, the generally stoical Murray still felt a lingering resentment. He told me that Walter Robins had promised him he would be on the plane.

Murray did, however, again prove his worth as the model professional who was prepared to play literally anywhere in the world by joining a Commonwealth side under the captaincy of Peter Richardson of Kent for five weeks in Pakistan late in 1963.

Richardson later remembered that he didn't want what he called 'second-division players' in his party. 'It's a state of mind,' he added. In a three-day match against the President's XI at Rawalpindi from 22–24 November Murray actually opened the bowling (with 0-11 off four overs) while Keith Andrew kept wicket. Before the teams went out for the third day's play they heard the news of President Kennedy's assassination in Dallas. The young Pakistani batsman Bashir Mian had tears in his eyes when Murray came in to bowl to him, although he still managed to score 64 before lunch. It seems safe to say that it was one of the few days of top-level competitive cricket ever played in Pakistan in complete silence, and they eventually called it off as a draw. Again demonstrating his have bag, will travel approach to his craft, Murray then joined an International Cavaliers side on a tour of the West Indies in the new year. This particular visit gave players and spectators a rare link back to the golden post-war age of English cricket, since no less than Godfrey Evans, now aged 43 and eking a living out of freelance bookmaking and ghosted journalism, was also in the side. I asked Murray about his illustrious predecessor. 'Still bloody sharp behind the stumps, a bit of a handful when he'd had a few drinks,' he told me. 'We had to take him back to the hotel in Kingston one night in a wheelbarrow.'

In 1964 the England Test match selection panel consisted of Walter Robins in the chair, assisted by Alec Bedser and Willie Watson, with Doug Insole, the former Essex captain, at 38 representing youth. While neither Bedser nor Watson was particularly keen on the idea of picking a wicketkeeper based largely on his batting, Insole thought otherwise; he felt that England would likely need all the runs they could get against that summer's touring Australians with their new-ball attack of Neil Hawke and Graham McKenzie, with the likes of Norman O'Neill in reserve, and, besides, how hard was it just to squat there halfway back to the boundary and more or less routinely catch the ball while wearing a pair of heavily-padded gloves? Insole himself was an occasional wicketkeeper, taking a couple of dozen catches along with six stumpings in the course of a 17-year first-class career, and later demonstrating a safe metaphorical pair of hands as a chairman of the TCCB and England tour manager.[2] Walter Robins for his part still had what amounted to a fetish for what he called 'brighter' cricket. Every individual selection and team strategy was subordinate to that ideal. Even E.W. Swanton, generally a man of plenipotentiary restraint when commenting on his cricket contemporaries born in the early days of the 20th century, later had this to say of Robins:

> 'He was impatient and disdainful of the safety-first ruts that the game had got into in the early 1960s, and some of the leading players, while agreeing maybe in their hearts with much that he said, found it too strong medicine. Most of

—

2 The sensational omission of Basil D'Oliveira from the 1968/69 MCC touring party to South Africa was far from the only headline-grabbing event of Insole's long tenure as an administrator. He was also the man behind Geoff Boycott's sacking by England after having scored a nine-and-a-half-hour unbeaten 246 in the Headingley Test against India in 1967. The selectors publicly chided the player's 'selfish batting'. Reflecting on this incident 40 years later, Boycott admitted to still feeling aggrieved at his treatment. Insole 'should have spelt his name with an "A",' he observed.

> us grow mellower, I suppose, with age, but poor Walter became if anything rather less so; in retrospect these early years of the 60s must have seen the first onset of the hardening of the brain arteries which after a long, and particularly distressing, illness proved fatal towards the end of the decade.'

Which is all to say that the classically-inclined Murray would have had his work cut out for him to successfully win back his place in the England team as it was constituted in 1964. For one reason or another, it was increasingly the era of the utility player who could dart off 30 runs and hold his own in the field rather than that of the stylist who might play the 'wrong' stroke at times but rarely if ever a truly clumsy one – the sort who invites spectators to delight in his inconsistency. Still, Murray made a bright enough start to the year when batting in a match against the county champions Yorkshire, with Fred Trueman, Brian Close and Ray Illingworth in the attack, on a winter-cold mid-May morning at Headingley. Going out to the middle before lunch with Middlesex on 71/5, he left again with his team on 309/6, having scored an unbeaten individual innings of 111 in just under three hours. Murray finished that particular season with 1,130 first-class runs, which included seven other scores of 50 or more, to go along with his 72 dismissals. Jim Parks played in all five Tests in the series against Australia, which the tourists took 1-0. Peter Burge effectively won the Ashes for his side when he scored 160 to help leave England 121 behind on the first innings at Leeds, a deficit from which the home team never recovered. Burge, whose all-action knock also took advantage of several missed catches, once remarked:

> 'We used to watch some of the England tactics that summer and wonder if they actually wanted to win the Ashes or just have a rollicking good knockabout for the crowd. I couldn't hit the old ball off the square that day at Leeds. Then there was a great powwow among the English fielders, with people jumping up and down and waving their arms at them from the dressing-room balcony, and lo and behold they took the new ball and we carted it all round the park.'

Ted Dexter was still the England captain that summer, and later wrote:

> 'The worst of it, the truly sad thing, was that we never quite trusted Mr Robins's judgement. He was a strange man, extremely generous, and at times brilliant in managing men but during his time as Chairman he just failed to win the confidence of his team.'

Of course it's not unusual for the England Test selectors to occasionally get things wrong, but some of the choices in both players and tactics from the years around 1960–65 begin to look almost wilfully misguided.

Towards the end of the 1964 season, Dexter perhaps whimsically decided that he would like to have a go at standing as the Tory candidate for the then solidly working-class Cardiff South-East in that October's general election. His opponent was Jim Callaghan, the future prime minister then serving as Labour's shadow chancellor, who had held the seat since the constituency was created in 1950. As a result, Dexter ruled himself out of the winter tour to South Africa, and the selectors named Warwickshire's 31-year-old Mike Smith to lead the side in his absence. Murray and Parks were the two chosen wicketkeepers. When the day of the election came, Callaghan increased his majority from 868 to just under 8,000. So Dexter decided he was free to tour after all, and travelled to South Africa as Smith's vice-captain. Parks again kept wicket throughout the series, which England won 1-0, although curiously enough Murray, having just scored 142 going in at number eight in a state match at Pretoria, was drafted in to the side as a specialist batsman for the fifth and final Test at Port Elizabeth. He made a total of 12 runs for once out, finishing with a healthy average for the tour of 36. I once asked him about the anomaly of his having played as a batsman for England while his primary rival kept wicket, and he answered modestly:

> 'I was a bloody odd choice to open the innings, because we all knew that John Edrich was playing club cricket in South Africa just then, and with a bit more thought somebody could have whistled him up.'

To add to the challenge of going in first on a green wicket against the likes of Peter Pollock and Trevor Goddard,

Murray's opening partner for the occasion was the young Geoff Boycott.

'Geoff was a great batsman, but let's just say he wasn't a warm and fuzzy bloke in those days. I went down to talk to him in between overs to ask if he had any particular advice to give me about the bowling, and you might as well have been enquiring who he fancied to be elected the next pope. "You're down your end, and I'm up my end, and that's all there is to it," he announced.'

After the Test, which was drawn, some of the players had a whip-round in order to take the former England captain Wally Hammond and his wife out to dinner. Hammond had emigrated to South Africa a decade earlier, but had since both lost his job and been involved in a serious car crash, events that perhaps served to further darken a personality already prone to the choleric. Although just 61, the once dashing Gloucestershire star was now a ponderous figure with slow eyes and a thin slot of a mouth.

'We got to the hotel,' Murray said, 'and there was Wally waiting for us. We all said a cheery hello and told him we had to nip in to another room to shake some hands, but that we'd be right out again, and then on our way to a slap-up dinner. When we got back 15 minutes later Wally was gone. He left a note for us with the hall porter. It said that he'd never been so insulted in all his life by our behaviour in making him wait for us. "I am a former captain of England and you buggers have dishonoured the office" was the gist of it. He died about four months later. All very sad.'

* * *

In January 1965, just as John Murray was representing MCC in their seven-wicket win over Orange Free State at Bloemfontein, I was one of the new intake at St Aubyns in our seaside fastness on the chalk cliffs of Rottingdean, an old smugglers' lair a couple of miles down the coast from Brighton. Looking back, the place had a sort of anticipatory touch of Hogwarts to it, if sadly lacking any of that fabled establishment's air of raw energy, vital social life and racy extracurricular activities. As mentioned, both the headmaster, the remote and forbidding Mr Gervis, and many of his subordinate team had been there in my father's day 30 years earlier. They shuffled around in impressively old thick tweed suits, worn whatever the season, some of them still displaying vestiges of their Edwardian-era youthful brilliance, others, it has to be said, barely qualified academically to do the job at all. Their young pupils lived under strict totalitarian vigilance. There were frequent daily assemblies and roll-calls, letters home were monitored, and morning visits to the lavatory were logged, and their physical results minutely inspected by an ancient matron wielding a clipboard. Food tended to be scarce and often inedible. I actually quite enjoyed the place. It offered the first real sense of stability in a life otherwise dictated by the need to move out of one nondescript naval housing estate and in to another one, sometimes thousands of miles away, every other year.

On Sunday mornings after chapel, Mr Gervis assembled everyone on long wooden benches in the schoolroom and read to us from an improving book. Over the years, I can remember generous helpings of everything from *The Pilgrim's Progress* to *The Screwtape Letters*, and at least one rousing declamation of Elizabeth I's words to her troops while awaiting the Spanish Armada. On national holidays, Mr Gervis sometimes treated us to John of Gaunt's speech from Act 2, Scene 1 of *Richard II*, his voice rising to a fever pitch of emotion as he reached the line about 'this blessed plot, this earth, this realm, this England'. To this day, I can never read the play without recalling those bitingly cold Sundays and that peak-decibel voice from the lectern. Shakespeare's language, as it was boomed out to us, seemed more like a mountain carved in to runnels and crags by time than like something man-made. There was, in the end, something that went beyond eloquence; there was something appalling about it.

As noted, there was also a large games field at St Aubyns, tilting down in a way that made the ridge at Lord's seem monotonously flat by comparison, with a small road at one end and the sea at the other. This was where I discovered cricket. Almost immediately I did so I became confident of achieving first-class honours. This was not a view shared by anyone else. My fielding skills were modest, and I still remember one of the masters remarking, not unkindly, that in his opinion there were really only two basic types of batsmen – those who moved their feet and played more or less straight, and those who just stood there, took a swipe at the ball, and hoped for the best. 'You define the latter category,' he told me.

I must have known at least something about cricket in general and Murray in particular even before then, because I find that I took the trouble to glue a team photograph of the

1964 Middlesex side in to my first term's school exercise book, and that I underlined the names in the caption both of Murray and his colleagues Eric Russell, Fred Titmus and John Price. Price was a talented fast bowler with an unusual approach to the wicket. Revving up from somewhere behind deep extra cover, his seemingly never-ending run eventually curved around the bend and on to a straight line, generating impressive speed en route. I remember that he had a cleft chin and was sadly injury-prone. At his best Price was thrilling to watch, and keeping to him sometimes seemed to carry Murray to impossibly distant regions, where his telescopic right arm would click out as he took the ball somewhere in front of the waiting slip cordon.

Another sign of latent cricket interest on my part came at about the time I went up to St Aubyns, when I happened to read that the MCC were holding an open day at Lord's, and that this was in some way a pre-sale opportunity to sign up for full-scale coaching classes to be held on the ground during the Easter holiday. I lobbied strongly to go, largely because of the tantalising prospect it seemed to offer of being able to gaze reverently at the Middlesex dressing-room. In the end we didn't make it to Lord's, although my parents did allow me a final, pre-boarding school fling by taking me to stand in the hushed crowd assembled outside the house near Hyde Park where Winston Churchill lay dying.

About four months later I was back in the St Aubyns schoolroom one early June morning, watching a few precious minutes of cricket on the tinny black-and-white set bolted to its wooden perch some 30 yards from where I sat in the obscurity of the junior back-benches. It was a Middlesex v Lancashire county championship match of the type which in those days you could still see on ordinary TV, and it was raining. I have a rather disjointed but unshakable memory of a tall, burly seamer coming in at a serpentine angle, and the right-handed batsman flashing outside his leg stump for an attempted on-drive, mistiming his shot in the gloom, and the ball corkscrewing off the outside edge back in the general direction of second slip. Murray, behind the stumps, had already begun to move the other way, and as I watched he somehow reversed thrust and took two or three scuttling steps to his right, impossibly fast, and then, diving, shot out a white-backed glove, landed on his feet, and kept running for a step or two more, until he was somewhere around the gully area. And then he was throwing the ball up in unfeigned delight and there was that familiar split-second of shocked silence before the crowd started applauding and the batsman looked around, suddenly and rather comically gave a shudder, as if having just been jolted by a cattle-prod, and then recovered himself and trudged off in the rain. I looked up the scorecard about 50 years later and read, *K. Goodwin, c Murray, b Price, 0.*

It had a certain ring to it.

# 4.
# GENTLEMAN

MURRAY turned 30 on 1 April 1965. He'd already been a full-time cricketer for 13 years, played in 15 Tests and toured all of the major countries. Now, professionally speaking, he was middle-aged. Murray's relative antiquity was well known on the county circuit – his opponents made it so – and now the combined birthday–April Fool's pranks that formed part of the Middlesex early spring training ritual were also an annual reminder, if one were necessary.

The regimen itself was on the rudimentary side. After the long winter layoff the Middlesex squad, for the most part overweight and undertrained, tended to just turn up, sign in with the club secretary, and then drift down the corridor for a cup of tea and a natter in the dressing-room. This latter sanctum was spartan, nondescript, and as slavishly functional as a dentist's reception area. A not-disagreeable smell of linseed oil and fresh paint generally wafted up from the pavilion railings. After that, the players might amble out for a gentle net. As a rule they would then go on to have a few drinks across the road in the Red Lion, perhaps followed by a curry, and finally pile in to a couple of cars to drop everyone off at their homes in places like Harrow or Isleworth. About two o'clock one morning, Fred Titmus drove a small group of team-mates back to Don Bennett's place in north London, where they watched their county's star all-rounder and sometime England Youth football international get out of the car and stagger up the path to his front door, which was part of a long row of identical red-brick houses. 'We drove off, and it turned out it wasn't Don's place after all,' Titmus said. 'He was sitting there over breakfast with some sales rep and his wife.' In those days Murray himself still usually cadged a lift or took the train back to 42 East Court in Wembley, where he joined Colleen and six-year-old Debbie and practised his true calling in life, which was for being a thoroughly devoted family man.

This same Titmus was now captain of Middlesex, taking over from the young Oxford University graduate Colin Drybrough, and as part of his duties he liked to give a short pep talk to the team in the dressing-room a day or two before the start of the new season. 'He told us to play hard, but also to try and entertain and all that stuff,' Murray remembered. 'Fred was a quiet motivator. When I look back, I can see why the guys would play their hearts out for him. He had that ability to get on you when you needed it, but he also had that pipe-smoking, laid-back side to him. The early 60s weren't a great era at Middlesex, but when the time came Fred really put his body and soul into it.' I once asked Murray how he felt about being consistently overlooked for the captaincy job himself, except on a caretaker basis. 'I was a little disenchanted,' he said.

In the event Titmus was down with the flu for several days in the immediate build-up to the 1965 season, and when the hour came it was Murray who stepped in to the breach to address the troops. His speech, if not touching the Sunday morning oratorical heights achieved by Mr Gervis in the St Aubyns schoolroom, was a modest *tour de force*. One of the players who was present told me that Murray applied the same principles in public speaking that he brought to the middle: directness, energy, simplicity and a fundamental optimism. 'He just spoke naturally. Nothing fancy. And once out [in the] nets it was a case of explanation, demonstration, imitation, correction, and then repetition, repetition, repetition. I'll never forget hour after hour of him crouching behind me, muttering things like "Front foot, mate ... " and "Elbow, son, *elbow* ... " after each ball. You listened, too, because you knew he'd seen it all.' When Murray was in charge of the team he always made it a point to tell his players every day that they were better than their opponents. Were they really? Not always. But in his mind, if they believed they were, then they were.

The 1965 season began for Murray on a sunny but bitterly raw Wednesday morning in late April when he donned the gauntlets and went out to represent the MCC against Yorkshire at Lord's. The thermometer aside, this was a promising start to the proceedings. Murray took his usual three catches in the one completed Yorkshire innings, and, according to *The Times*, 'batted beautifully off back and front foot, scoring freely in all sectors' before being bowled by, of all people, Geoff Boycott. But that wasn't really what mattered. For Murray, the outstanding fact of the match was simply that he was back in what amounted to a full-strength England team, and the likes of Smith, Andrew and Parks weren't. Doug Insole was now the chairman of selectors, and told the press his primary task was to pick the 'eleven best specialist players' for the season's twin three-match Test series against New Zealand and South Africa. (He actually used the word *specialist*.) So it was no wonder when, speaking to a reporter from the London *Evening News* later in May, Murray himself sounded upbeat. 'You never know about [England] selection,' he said, truly enough. 'But I feel I'm playing as well as I ever have. I'm ready.'

But if publicly Murray put up a bold front, the same paper noting his 'hearty laugh, his mile-wide smile and the gleam in his eye', in private it was another matter. 'I sometimes felt I was knocking on Insole's door, but nobody was home,' he once told me.

Following the MCC match, Murray drove up with the Middlesex team to a windswept Cambridge and promptly scored 106 against the university. Nothing particularly stellar in that, perhaps, but the innings left a big impression on the students' captain Ray White, also of Gloucestershire and Transvaal. 'I remember Murray pulled one ball from outside the off stump and on a good length to the square-leg rope. It hit a wooden board there and shot halfway back to the middle.' Just to prove it was no fluke, the next week Murray was back at Lord's scoring a breezy 51 against Notts while 'Bomber' Wells tied the other batsmen to their creases. The home side eventually won a game that could still have gone either way when Don Bennett wheeled in to bowl the last over. *The Times* wrote: 'Murray's batting so far this year has displayed power, grace and many runs. He is at the peak of his form.'

Twenty-three-year-old Mike Brearley, who opened the Middlesex batting that season, later remarked of his county team-mate: 'At his best, JT was a wonderfully fluent player, especially against fast bowling – he was a fine hooker – and against spin, where he used his feet and hit beautifully over the top.' But, to Brearley, Murray was always a better bet for the brilliant cameo innings than the patient, all-day one. 'John saw himself as a wicketkeeper first and a batsman second … For a man with such talent, he was too often bowled through the gate, or by just missing a straight ball.' Brearley added: 'He was less likely to succeed against bowlers he regarded as blatantly second-rate.'

Ten years earlier, Denis Compton had strolled out to the Nursery End nets at Lord's one bright April morning and stood there watching the young Murray taking batting practice against the lively medium-pace pair of Bill Edrich and Alan Moss. 'John was fast on his feet, but he had something more important than that,' Compton later recalled. 'He was fearless. Like most people, when the bowlers put the ball under his nose – remember no one bothered with crash-helmets back then – he pulled his head back. I told him if he learned to hold still and hook the short ball it would make him a better all-round player – it takes the wind out of the bowler's sails.'

Compton also went on to agree that it takes a certain amount of inner steel to stay in line while a rock-hard cricket ball rears off a length and shoots towards your unprotected head, particularly when the man batting immediately before you has just been struck on the bridge of his nose and been helped away from the net by two concerned colleagues, his blood staining the grass, as had been the case that particular spring morning with Middlesex's Harry Sharp.

'John was a quick study,' Compton said admiringly. 'It was a duck to water. Once he got the mechanics down that shot brought him a ton of runs.'

In the middle of May 1965 Murray was chosen to play for the MCC against New Zealand at a funereally dark-skied Lord's. He did everything right, including pulling off a leaping one-handed catch to dismiss the left-handed Bert Sutcliffe while standing up to the brisk if also somewhat random seam bowling of Richard Hutton on a wet wicket, a combination presenting something of the same assorted challenges of the man fumbling for his front door key while simultaneously being weighed down by heavy shopping and harassed by the house cat. There were no byes in either New Zealand innings. The match was called off as a draw in the sea-grey evening light of Tuesday 18 May. Four days later, Insole and his co-selectors announced the team to represent England in the first Test at Edgbaston. Parks was the wicketkeeper.

As usual, Murray took the news in his stride, masking his obvious disappointment with humour. Not only was he admirably sanguine about his longer-term Test prospects, but he assumed the selectors were more objective and open-minded than they really were. Asked to describe the difference between Parks and himself by a rather earnest young reporter from the

Indian newspaper *The Pioneer*, Murray said, 'Jim has a thick head of hair and I don't' – 'a very solemn and sincere statement', the reporter believed, quoting it as such in his article.

While England were trouncing New Zealand at Edgbaston, Murray stood in in Titmus's absence as captain of Middlesex in their championship match with Somerset at Lord's. Like all too many games in that depressingly damp summer, it ended as a rain-soaked draw. One of the few reporters who bothered to notice the match wrote that there was something 'magnificently military' about Murray in his stance and turnout. 'He leapt like Gordon Banks to dispose of [Somerset opener] Atkinson off the bowling of Hooker, but then immediately returned to the vertical, standing as neat and erect as if on parade, acknowledged the applause with a curt nod, and then waited at attention for the next man in.'

In Mike Brearley's 1976 assessment published in *Wisden*:

> 'When Murray had the chance, he liked to attack. I remember once that he placed eight men around M.J.K. Smith on a placid pitch, and the ruse worked. Smith padded up to Price and was lbw for nought. At the same time he was fairly conventional in his ideas about tactics and field-settings.
>
> 'He had strong views about the spirit in which the game should be played, which included looking to get on top whether batting or fielding, and unquestioning acceptance of the umpire's decision. It's a nice question whether Murray might have been an outstanding county captain as well as

> everything else. I believe he was unlucky not to have had the chance.'

On 23 June Middlesex beat Sussex in the Gillette Cup quarter-final at Lord's. Nothing sensational in that, admittedly, although it happened to be the first ever defeat Sussex had suffered in the competition since its launch nearly three years earlier. Murray was named man of the match. He scored 49 in half an hour and then threw in his usual quota of three catches, including – giving the press its revenge narrative – one to dismiss Jim Parks, which he took low down in front of first slip. The next day Ted Dexter, the Sussex captain, decompressed by driving himself in his new metallic-blue Jaguar to Newbury racecourse. On the way back to London, the car ran out of petrol. Instead of waiting for assistance, Dexter pushed the Jag to a nearby garage. Unfortunately, he lost control and it ended up pinning him to the gates of a champagne distribution warehouse, breaking his right leg. It was a serious injury, although mixed in with the widespread expressions of concern there was also a certain amount of dark humour, precisely because it seemed to be the sort of thing that happened to Dexter rather than to normal cricketers. He had just turned 30, and other than a brief, unhappy comeback in 1968 his Test career was now over. Mike Smith led England to win the series against New Zealand and to lose the one that followed with South Africa.

Murray was again captain when Middlesex went up to play Yorkshire at Scarborough at the end of July. The match represented an individual success for him set amidst a collective failure by the team. Middlesex reached 131/1 in their first innings, but then folded to 150 all out, Fred Trueman taking 5-32. Yorkshire replied with 373. This time, Murray took four catches. The visitors were then quickly 59/4, still 164 behind, when, wearing a freshly starched white shirt and an expression of grim determination, their captain came to the crease. His match-saving unbeaten 132 struck *The Times* correspondent as 'brilliant', if at the same time 'gratuitously pugnacious [in the way] he unleashed a flood of drilling strokes against Trueman at his fastest'. Murray laughed when I once asked him about the 'gratuitously pugnacious' bit. 'It looked like Middlesex were going to be thumped on the Thursday afternoon, which would have given everyone an extra day off. So there was going to be a big golf match and a piss-up for the players and writers on the Friday. I managed to bugger all that up for them.'

On the few occasions when Murray wasn't scoring runs that season he was busy adding to his haul of dismissals – nine of them, eight caught, one stumped, in the game against Hampshire at Lord's. He dropped one there, too, characteristically then just picking the ball up and throwing it back without comment. Part of his charm was that he was never merely robotically efficient in the field. Nobody, least of all Murray himself, ever said he was infallible. The great thing about his personal triumphs, like the one against Hampshire, was that you always felt you were watching a human being in action, not just a catching machine, albeit a rather superior member of the species who rarely if ever seemed to be hurried or off-balance, even when the ball once hit a crack in the pitch and took off over the batsman's left shoulder, forcing Murray to alter course, dance backwards towards the vacant fine-leg position, reach up, pull the ball down, glare at it for a moment as if in rebuke for having troubled him, then smoothly pass it back down the line again, having saved a certain four byes in the process.

In early August, Murray captained Middlesex in their championship match against Surrey at Lord's. He top-scored with 98 in the first innings, having tried to put the slow left-armer Roger Harman in to the grandstand to bring up his ton, but getting an inside edge on to his stumps instead. Shortly afterwards, the MCC selectors announced the names of the 16 players to tour Australia under Mike Smith's captaincy that winter. Murray and Parks were the wicketkeepers. Later in the season Smith led an England XI against the Rest of the World at Scarborough. Excessive heat is rarely a factor in autumnal English domestic cricket, but perversely enough it was scorching on the first day of play, warm and windy on the second, and torrentially wet on the third. Murray, though back as the de facto Test wicketkeeper, barely got on the field. His last match of the season was for an MCC team led by Fred Titmus taking on a full-strength Yorkshire side under Brian Close. Murray scored 21 in the first innings and 80 not out in the second. When all the figures were added up he had 1,160 first-class runs for the season at an average of just under 30. Middlesex again finished sixth in the table, marking their 16th year of delayed gratification since last winning the title.

* * *

As Murray was sitting with the other MCC players in their navy blazers and grey flannels over a rather sparse set breakfast in their anonymous west London hotel immediately prior to flying off (economy class) to Australia on Saturday, 16 October 1965, he spotted a mildly familiar face across the dining room. It belonged to S.C. 'Billy' Griffith, the 51-year-old former Surrey, Sussex and occasional England wicketkeeper who was serving as the tour manager. Murray had shaken Griffith's hand once or twice in the past, but he barely knew him and assumed that Griffith didn't know him either. 'He was one of those smooth blokes in suits you occasionally met in the corridor at Lord's,' Murray told me, adding that Griffith had also appeared during the previous MCC tour of Australia when the Duke of Norfolk had found it expedient to fly home for a month, either for the officially-given 'reasons of state' (organising the rehearsal for Winston Churchill's funeral, for one thing) or, as some of the cricketers believed, because he simply preferred spending Christmas at home on his country estate rather than in a succession of one-star hotels in places like Tasmania.

This somewhat threadbare prior social acquaintance would now become a rather strained professional relationship. Murray also knew that Griffith had been 'a useful bat and at least a capable keeper' in the immediate post-war years. Their first-class careers had even overlapped for a season or two in the early 1950s. It might be going too far, but not, perhaps, going totally in the wrong direction to say that Griffith was the Jim Parks figure of his day. Like Parks he was essentially a one-day batsman who could also competently catch the ball in his gloves if called upon to do so. He had no pretension to any great style or polish behind the stumps, and Godfrey Evans long remembered his surprise, to put it no stronger than that, on his being replaced by Griffith for the last two Tests of the 1948/49 MCC tour of

South Africa. (Evans always believed that his omission had more to do with his *faux pas* in having playfully poured a glass of beer over the imposing head of Brigadier Green, the tour manager, than it did any technical lapses on the field.) Anyway, Griffith – who it should be noted was also a bona fide war hero – was one of those thoroughly sound gentleman cricketers who went on to a long and distinguished administrative career, as well as being a natural conciliator who preferred to let others take the more unpleasant decisions.

When Griffith sat down next to Murray over their soggy toast and tinned orange juice that Saturday morning in October 1965 he was joined by his friend Doug Insole, the chairman of selectors, the latter 'beaming about a million volts of toothy charm', I was later told. The two men were working the room with a simple message that they wished to impress on each of the 15 players. (Titmus was ill, and flew out to Australia later.) It was that, whatever else happened, the English cricketers should go about their business in the most positive and attractive way possible. All else was secondary to that transcendent principle. Murray never forgot Griffith's exact choice of phrase on the subject: 'I want to see the runs gushing out from your bat like oil from a fresh strike' – oddly enough, precisely the same evocative term that *Wisden* later used in its published report of the Test series, which England went on to draw with Australia one-all. 'I don't know why, but at that moment I somehow got the feeling that it was going to be more Parks's tour than mine,' Murray remembered thinking as he prepared to leave home for the next five months.

It has to be said that Griffith's high starting hopes for the tour were never quite fulfilled on a practical basis. The early upcountry games went well enough, and even Geoff Boycott followed instructions when he finally went out to play his maiden innings of the tour – he'd been one of several players to go down with a mystery virus shortly after arrival – to hit the first ball he faced in Australia for four. But the reality of a long Ashes series seems to have set in by about the time the tourists reached Melbourne in the middle of November, where Ken Barrington dug in for what was described as 'an innings of rugged, fighting grandeur' that produced 158 runs, but also proved one of those unsatisfactory affairs for all but the most partisan English supporter, in which classical style was matched by a careful, gritty application on the batsman's part. Six months earlier, Barrington had taken 437 minutes to score 137 against a mediocre New Zealand attack at Edgbaston, almost bringing the game to a standstill in the process. Coming in at 54-1 he spent an hour without scoring, before going on to suddenly emerge from an apparent coma a day later to hit two fours and a six in a single over to bring up his century. Although England won by nine wickets Barrington was dropped for slow scoring, and Insole wrote to him to say:

> 'We acted more in sorrow than in anger in leaving you out of the side for Lord's. I think our feeling is that it is the only practical way of demonstrating that we are not prepared to condone cricket of the Edgbaston variety.'

Murray was one of those who believed that his friend Barrington, one of life's inveterate worriers, never quite recovered from this blow to his self-confidence, if anything becoming a worse batsman, not a better one, as a result. 'There was always that nagging doubt in the back of Kenny's mind from then on, and you saw him getting out to shots that he never would have played without the extra pressure he felt on him from the selectors. It did his head in. That was the reality of "brighter cricket".' Nor was this a concept necessarily embraced by the Australians or their hatchet-faced captain Bill Lawry, a man whose own core batting technique once won him the derisive description of a 'corpse with pads on'. By the time MCC met Victoria at Melbourne the gaudy optimism that had characterised the early press forecasts that the series would be played in a spirit of unfailing enterprise and mutual goodwill had long since evaporated. In that same game where Barrington scored 158, Murray watched Lawry dislodge the bails with the heel of his boot and then calmly set off for a single. 'I appealed, but the umpire said not out. He hadn't seen what happened, and Lawry wasn't about to walk. I stumped the bugger later, though,' Murray chuckled.

* * *

'J.T. Murray made an excellent impression throughout Australia,' Griffith later wrote for the record in his official report on the tour. When given the chance he 'kept wicket admirably well, catch[ing] everything that came to him'. Batting for MCC against South Australia at Adelaide over Christmas week 1965, Murray also top-scored over the likes of Smith, Cowdrey and Barrington with a counter-attacking innings of 110. 'In the power and cleanness of his hitting, he looked the equal of any batsman in the world,' the *Advertiser* wrote. Geoff Boycott added that 'the whole tour was a slog, with people sharing poky little hotel rooms, no money to speak of, not even a doctor on call when you got sick, which most of us did – and through it all my memory is of John being permanently friendly and cheerful. He knew how to get along with people, even with some of the Aussies who could be irascible and uptight. He was a good tourist. He was also a great keeper, and when he batted he batted elegantly. You were always glad to have him in the side.'

The more Murray was kicked around by the England selectors, the more genial and beatifically laid-back he seemed to become. He was most in his element somewhere like the small park at Euroa, 90 miles upcountry from Melbourne, where the MCC match with a Victoria XI had to be suspended after heavy rain, and the journalist E.M. Wellings watched as the visitors' wicketkeeper then spent most of the afternoon signing autographs and offering priceless coaching tips to a horde of young Australian admirers – 'beaming the whole time as he did so'. Perhaps he was thinking of his wife and young daughter back home in north London. Parks again played in all five of the Tests against Australia that winter. He finished with the highly creditable series batting average of 48, though the critics were divided when it came to other aspects of his game. Wellings later wrote in *Wisden*:

> 'Parks batted so well and so aggressively that he was worth selection as a specialist batsman ... He saved the side in the first Test and came off with the bat in each subsequent one except the third. The pity was that he was also required to keep wicket

> throughout, though Murray was so obviously his superior.
>
> 'Parks's blunder in missing a simple off-side chance of stumping Burge off Barber almost certainly cost England the second Test and with it the Ashes ... It was unfortunate that one of the main tour successes should be thus so crucially at fault. The blame rather should rest with selectors who would not appreciate that bowlers deserve the best possible wicket-keeper irrespective of any other consideration.'

As a result of all this Murray again settled in to the job of Parks's tour understudy, a role that involved some enjoyable travel, a little cricket and a lot of golf, wine and unstinting public relations work. He was also one of the few tourists who managed to stay fully match-fit throughout the five-month trek, which Boycott (who at one point had to be left behind, 'chucking my guts up', in a Singapore hotel room) remembers as 'like *Emergency Ward 10*, but without the doctors'. Now down to barely a quorum of fit players, the Englishmen arrived in Christchurch late in February 1966 to begin the three-Test series with New Zealand. Ironically, Parks had one of his best-ever matches behind the stumps there, taking a total of eight catches. What was ironic about it was that the selectors then promptly dropped him. Murray came back for the second Test, at Dunedin, and also did well, with four catches in the one completed New Zealand innings and a thumping 50 (three fours and two sixes) when batting in the middle order. He, in turn, was dropped, and Parks came back for the final Test at Auckland. Like its predecessors, it, too, was drawn. While Parks then went off on his honeymoon, the remaining English tourists flew on to Hong Kong and from there to London, which they reached late in the afternoon of 21 March. Having left home before the autumn leaves had fallen and returned again on the first day of spring, Murray earned £782 (inclusive of a £50 good-merit bonus) for his winter's work, a rate of slightly under £5 a day.

* * *

Even in the mid-1960s an annual salary of something like £2,000 didn't go far in London. After 14 years as a professional cricketer, Murray was doing slightly better than the average unskilled worker, who around then was taking home £22 a week, and certainly had more in the bank than his father Jim did at a comparable age. But it was still a pittance to show for one of England's best-known international sportsmen. Murray never complained, but once told me he never felt himself wholly secure, either, 'and while you were going out to play in a Test in front of 30,000 people somewhere in the back of your mind you were also worrying about the gas bill waiting for you at home'.[3]

So it was welcome news when the Middlesex committee voted Murray a benefit season in 1966. A dozen Sunday afternoon all-star games and several dinners and raffles later

3 I once came across a small and touching example of this when Murray handed me a letter from the MCC which had invited him to go on a major overseas tour. Pencilled in on the back were several immaculately neat rows of projected income and expenses for the trip, once or twice punctuated by a question mark or other note of concern in his own hand.

and he was some £8,000 richer, which may not have been in the later Geoff Boycott or Graeme Hick testimonial-year class, but at least proved useful when it came to paying the mortgage in north Wembley.

Murray wrote in the preface to his fundraising brochure, in terms which possibly owed something to an editor: 'During my association with the Middlesex club there has always been a great desire to entertain the watching public. This I have tried to do, how successful I have been is for you to judge,' before going on from there to thank an impressive array of county officials and colleagues. About 50 years after he put his name to these words, Murray told me that the real unsung hero of the day was the old Kent batsman and occasional keeper James Seymour, who had died in 1930. Seymour grossed about £900 from his own 1920 benefit season, and later fought the Inland Revenue all the way up to the House of Lords over how much of this windfall he might actually be allowed to keep. Their lordships' final ruling said: 'We do not feel compelled by any of the authorities to hold that an employer cannot make a solitary gift to his employee without rendering the gift liable to taxation', a principle that prominent English cricketers still apply today, every time they bank £400,000 or £500,000 for a benefit season. 'Old Seymour was a true British hero,' Murray told me with a straight face one day. 'Somebody should write a book about him.'

* * *

Swinging London's pendulum began to gently tick back and forth in 1966, with such eye-catching developments as sexually liberated young women swaggering down King's Road with their shiny plastic go-go boots and Union Jack shopping bags, and the Rolling Stones performing their slightly disturbing new single 'Paint It, Black' on *Top of the Pops* – with the Second World War symbolically laid to rest when, in late July, England beat West Germany to win the World Cup – but in general terms the nation's first-class cricket scene remained serenely unruffled by the white-hot technological and cultural revolution breaking out all around it. London may suddenly have become the style capital of Europe, where fashion designers, models and photographers flocked, hair lengthened, skirts shortened, and a spirit of individual licence replaced the collective protocol of army life, but back on the county circuit, as Murray fondly remembered, it was still a case of 'a couple of slices of cold ham for lunch and a damp bed-and-breakfast hotel in Clacton for the weekend'.

The West Indies, under Garry Sobers, were popular and attractive visitors in what proved to be yet another dismally wet English summer in 1966. The virility and gaiety of their team lingered long in the minds of the 700,000 or so spectators who saw them in one or more of their 35 fixtures. A full house turned up at Arundel at the end of April to watch the tourists in their first match against a Duke of Norfolk's XI, for whom Tom Graveney, inexplicably out of favour with the Test selectors for the past three years, stroked his way to 58 before discreetly allowing himself to be bowled. Murray got his chance two weeks later, when he was chosen for the MCC side against the West Indies at Lord's. Going out on the second morning to face a fast bowling attack again spearheaded by Charlie Griffith and Wes Hall, with Lance Gibbs and Sobers himself in support, he scored an unbeaten innings of exactly 100, which was more than the top four men in the order managed between them. Sobers told me that when the time came, 'John [also] caught everything that was within reach, and a lot that was well out of reach too. If you'd taken a poll in the West Indies dressing-room we would have told you that Tom Graveney was the best batsman in England, and that Murray was by a mile the best wicketkeeper.' Nine days after the MCC match, Doug Insole and his co-selectors announced their team for the first Test at Old Trafford. Neither Murray nor Graveney was chosen.

Ten weeks later, the West Indies had beaten England in three of the first four Tests and drawn the other one, and it was time for one of those statistically meaningless but spirited fightbacks we seem to do better than any other sporting nation. The scene was the Oval, and for once the sun shone brightly as the new England captain Brian Close went out to toss with Sobers on the morning of 18 August. The 35-year-old Close, at one time the *enfant terrible* of post-war domestic cricket, and still England's youngest-ever Test player, was the third man to lead his country that summer. Mike Smith and Colin Cowdrey had each in turn been sacked, and the team at the Oval showed five changes from the one that had lost by an innings a week earlier at Leeds. In batting order, it read: Boycott, Barber, Edrich, Graveney, Amiss, D'Oliveira, Close, Illingworth, Murray, Higgs, Snow. Murray long remembered the pre-match dinner. 'Brian got up, fag in hand, slowly looked us up and down, and said: "I wouldn't be here if we hadn't made such a balls-up of the series. What's more, neither would most of you. I had you sent for because you're all fighters, and whatever else happens we're going to fight these buggers tooth and nail for the next five days." It might sound corny now, but I can tell you everyone sat up in their seats,' Murray added.

Alex Bannister of the *Daily Mail* interviewed Murray in the downstairs library in the Oval pavilion about 90 minutes before the start of play. There may be no atmosphere quite like that of a sold-out cricket ground with the hum of arriving spectators and the clatter of players' boots on the first morning of a Test match. 'England, as you may have noticed, haven't had a really proper wicketkeeper for years,' Bannister, the paper's cricket correspondent since 1947, observed. 'Let's face it, we've picked a lot of goalies to do the job, all nice chaps, who should never have been allowed near the Test team.

'Why have the selectors consistently ignored the best man for the job?'

Murray said he understood Bannister's concern. He assumed a tone of empathy as he responded in gentle buzzwords. 'I can only keep doing my best, Alex, and hope to be ready when the call comes.'

'Does this mark the beginning of your Test comeback?'

'Let's just focus on stuffing the West Indies here,' said Murray, 'and see what the future holds.' The other journalists dotted around the room laughed, except the intrepid *Mail* reporter.

'You're not thinking ahead to touring Australia again, John?'

'I'm only thinking ahead to next Tuesday,' Murray said.

The raw facts of the match are that the West Indies won the toss, batted, and scored 268. Rohan Kanhai made 104 and Sobers added 81. No one else got over 30. England were in some bother in their reply when, at 166/7, Murray joined Tom Graveney halfway through the second day. You could argue that they were the two most aggrieved parties to all the English selection follies of the 1960s. In an age preoccupied with accountancy they'd sometimes underperformed statistically, but rarely disappointed those who like a touch of the classical, and also occasionally the fallible, to their cricketers. Only mediocrity is always at its best. Murray, having survived an almighty shout for lbw first ball, scored 112, with 13 fours, in just over four hours at the crease. Graveney made 165, and their 217-run stand still remains an eighth-wicket record for England against the West Indies. Garry Sobers once told me that the greatest compliment he could pay Murray was that 'when you looked from Tom to John, and then back again, it was bloody difficult to tell them apart. Everything that could be hit they hit hard and straight.' The partnership ended only when, on the third day, Graveney played a shot to gully, Murray's prudent shout of 'No!' was lost in all the ambient Saturday-lunchtime din of hooters and klaxons, and the batsman was run out. 'Frankly, we could have batted all day,' Murray said, 'and the end, when it came, had to be self-inflicted.' The Oval scoreboard was soon spinning like a fruit machine again as Ken Higgs and John Snow then followed up with a last-ditch stand of 128, and England had a first innings lead of 259.

West Indies came out to bat a second time. The openers had both gone again within 20 minutes, each caught behind, and Close then enhanced his reputation for blue-sky thinking by advising Snow to bowl Garry Sobers a first-ball bouncer, which Sobers duly lobbed straight into the hands of Close himself at short leg. 'Brian was probably the best captain on the field I ever played with,' Murray once told me. 'He led from the front, never flinched, solid as a rock. With Cowdrey there was always this faint air of regret if England happened to get on top. He never wanted to turn the screw that last notch. It was bad form. Closey was just the opposite. It wasn't enough to win, you had to destroy the other buggers, really humiliate them.' Close himself once remarked, 'I can see the jugular in anyone and go for it, but I always keep myself in rein … I keep myself in rein, just like you would an animal.' According to Murray, the first part of that boast was accurate, but not the second. 'Much as I admired him as a captain, some people thought Closey a bit of a twat – what you'd politely call "opinionated", and among his opinions was the one that had himself as the Muhammad Ali of the cricket world, and everyone else, team-mates and opponents alike, as just a lot of lightweights.'

England bowled the West Indies out for 225 in their second innings at the Oval, winning the Test by an innings and 34 runs. Murray had scored his first international century, passed 11,000 runs in first-class cricket in the process, and put in an all-round performance that was as dominating as it was graceful. It was the supreme moment of vindication for a man somehow overlooked or ignored by the national selectors for much of the previous three years, whom *The Times* believed 'evinced a style both when batting and in the field that placed him in the loftiest company … surely only in England could a player of such undoubted skill ever be treated with mistrust' (and Close himself more succinctly hailed as 'fucking brilliant').

With the nation's applause still ringing in his ears, Murray had simply driven himself home on the Saturday evening of the Test and had what he called a 'completely normal, quiet night in

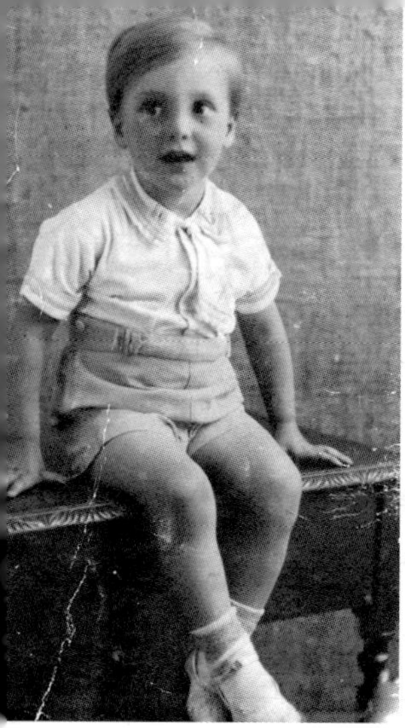

*West End boy.*

*Godfrey Evans, England's inimitable wicketkeeper during much of the 1950s.*

*Bill Edrich: An early influence, usually for the good, on Murray's career.*

*Denis (l) and Leslie Compton.*

*Tommy Lawton, the legendary England centre forward and later player-manager at Brentford who arrived unannounced one Sunday morning to offer the teenaged Murray professional terms.*

*Fresh-faced county hopeful.*

*Having just turned 17, keeping for Middlesex against Yorkshire at Lord's, June 1952. Len Hutton, seen here, scored 132 for the visitors.*

*Murray on his wedding day to Colleen Bryan, September 1958.*

*Baptism by fire: the ball flies off Alan Davidson's pads and hits the new England wicketkeeper above the eye – first Test against Australia at Edgbaston, June 1961.*

*Narrowly failing to run out Bill Lawry later in the 1961 series.*

*Murray with his Middlesex and England colleague Peter Parfitt on board the SS* Canberra*, bound for Australia. [Photo: Peter Parfitt]*

*Diligently leading a pre-breakfast run around the* Canberra*, while others preferred a quick smoke below decks.*

*Hurt again, after taking a spectacular catch in the third Test at Sydney, January 1963.*

*Poolside with his great friend and colleague Fred Titmus. Short, compact and chirpy, Titmus kept up a non-stop flow of chatter while in the field, sometimes when actually in the process of bowling. He later lost four toes of his left foot in a boating accident.*

*John Murray and Deryck Murray compare wicketkeeping notes before the start of a match between the Duke of Norfolk's XI and West Indies at Arundel, April 1963.*

*Jim Parks and Ted Dexter, two major players in Murray's England career, go out to bat for Sussex.*

*One that got away: Murray missing an errant throw from the field, in a county match against Yorkshire at Lord's, 1963. He still took five catches in the one completed Yorkshire innings.*

*The Middlesex contingent meet at Lord's before flying off with the 1964/65 MCC party to South Africa. L-r: John Price, Peter Parfitt, Fred Titmus, Mike Brearley, Murray and physio Richard Nicholas.*

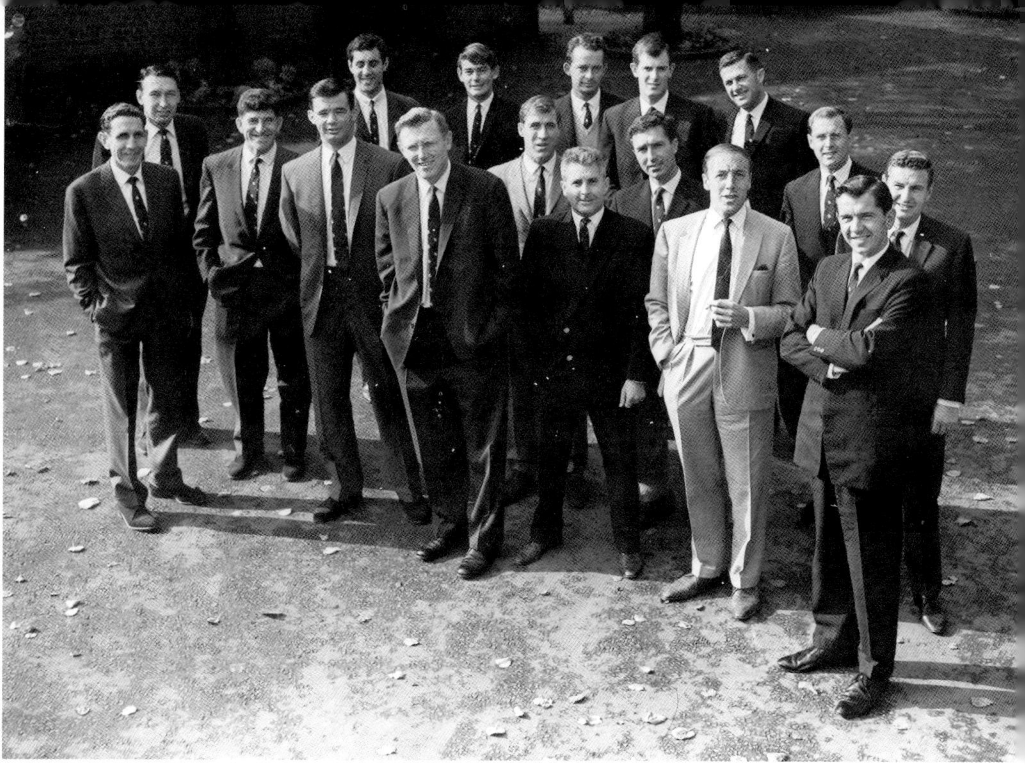

*The full tour party, captained by Mike (MJK) Smith. Ted Dexter flew out to join them later, after failing to be elected an MP.*

*Hitting out for Middlesex against Kent at Lord's, May 1965, while Colin Cowdrey and a young Alan Knott look on.*

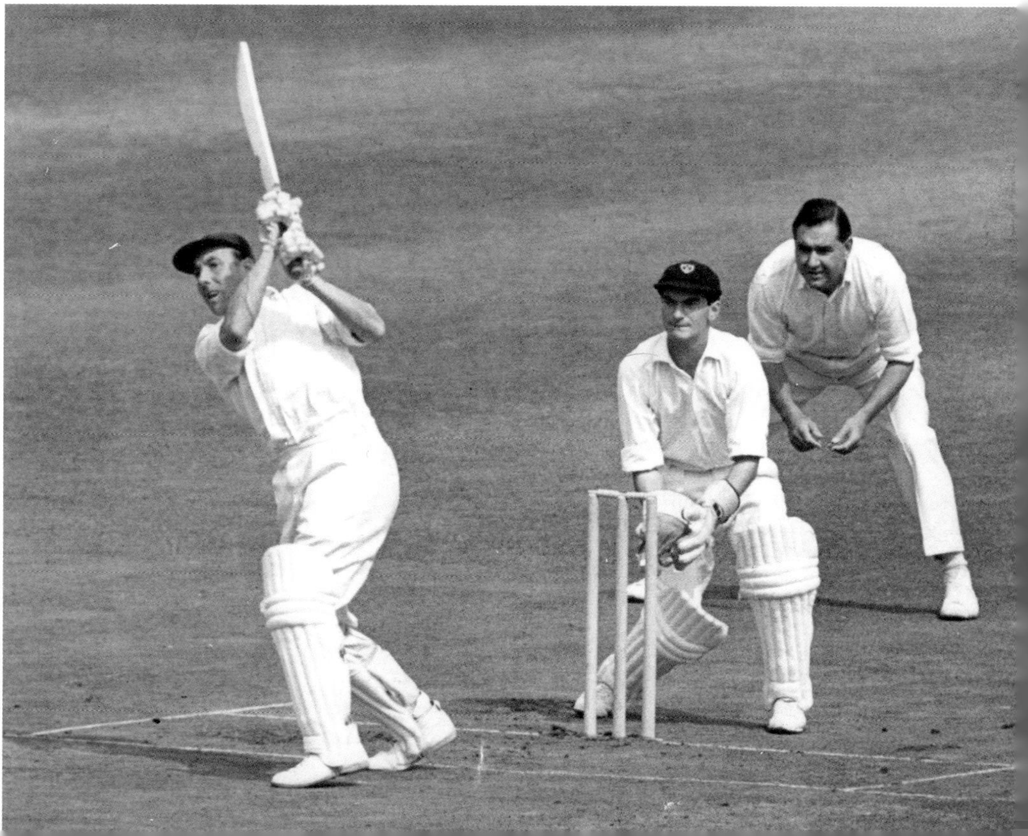

*Proving it was no fluke, winning the man-of-the-match award after scoring a brisk 49, and throwing in three catches, in the following month's Gillette Cup tie against Sussex.*

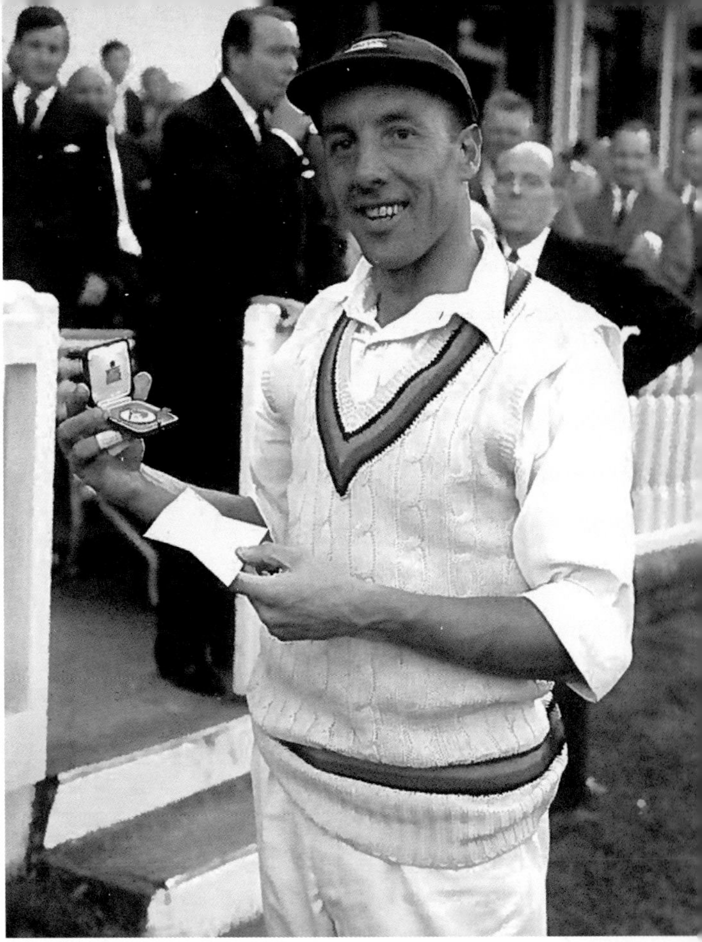

*Happy times: Fred Trueman prays before facing his first ball on a seaming wicket at Lord's. The fielders see the funny side.*

*The England side that beat the West Indies at the Oval in August 1966. Standing l-r: Boycott, Edrich, D'Oliveira, Snow, Amiss, Barber. Seated: Illingworth, Graveney, Close (capt), Murray, Higgs.*

*Murray walking off for a quick cup of tea and a cigarette during his innings of 112 in the same match. Note Garry Sobers's reaction.*

*The author (seated, second from right) looking suitably unhappy in a St Aubyns rugby team.*

*His ultimate role model at the time.*

*Barrington bats, with the Middlesex Test trio of Parfitt, Titmus and Murray behind.*

*The England team which beat India by an innings at Lord's in late June 1967. Standing, l-r: Edrich, Hobbs, Snow, Brown, D'Oliveira, Amiss. Seated: Barrington, Graveney, Close (capt), Murray, Illingworth. Murray did everything right in the match, including taking a record six catches in an innings. A month later England dropped him.*

*Alan Knott, a fine wicketkeeper-batsman who nonetheless struck some of Murray's more ardent supporters as a sort of stylised burlesque act.*

*Murray and Clive Radley shout for lbw off Fred Titmus's bowling: a characteristic sight of Middlesex cricket from about 1965–75.*

*Murray for once flat on his back.*

Telegrams :
LORD'S GROUND LONDON
Telephone Nos. :
Pavilion ... ... ... 01-289-1611-5
Tennis Court ... ... 01-289-1288
Tavern Caterers 01-286-2909
Works Dept. ... ... 01-286-6855
Prospects of Play ... 01-286-8011

Secretary :
S. C. GRIFFITH
Assistant Secretaries :
J. G. DUNBAR D. B. CARR
J. A. BAILEY

*Marylebone Cricket Club,*
*Lord's Ground,*
*London, N.W.8*

FT/P/C/SB 27th February, 1969

Dear Mrs. Murray,

I thought you would be interested to know that I have just received the following message, via the Foreign Office, from Mr. Les Ames, the Manager of the M.C.C. team, in Dacca:

"Rather worried what may appear in today's Press and consequent distress it could give to players' families. Amazing as it may seem, the smooth running of this Test Match depends upon the student leaders. I have interviewed them with the Captain and Deputy High Commissioner and feel they could be successful, and I have told them that if there is any trouble we shall withdraw. In any event, I am satisfied that the safety of the team is assured."

I am sure you will be as relieved as we are to know that the situation appears to be reasonably satisfactory.

Yours sincerely,

S C Griffith

Secretary, T.C.C.B.

Mrs. J.T. Murray

*'Nothing went right with England's 1968-69 plans,'* Wisden *remarked, although this letter from the MCC sought to put the best face on that winter's Pakistan tour fiasco.*

Greg Chappell hits one over midwicket while scoring a century for Australia in a World Cup warm-up game against Middlesex in May 1975. Murray, whose benefit match it was, stumped Chappell in the end. When the roles came to be reversed, the Australian captain, in keeping with cherished cricketing tradition, told his fast bowler Jeff Thomson to let Murray 'have one'. Thomson responded with a bouncer.

Batting for Middlesex in the 1975 Gillette Cup Final against Lancashire. It was Murray's final season, and he went out in front of a full house at Lord's.

*Keeping for the Duchess of Norfolk's XI against the touring Australians at Arundel, April 1977. Now aged 42, Murray still had what it took: 'any ball the batsman missed would melt into his hands,' a critic wrote.*

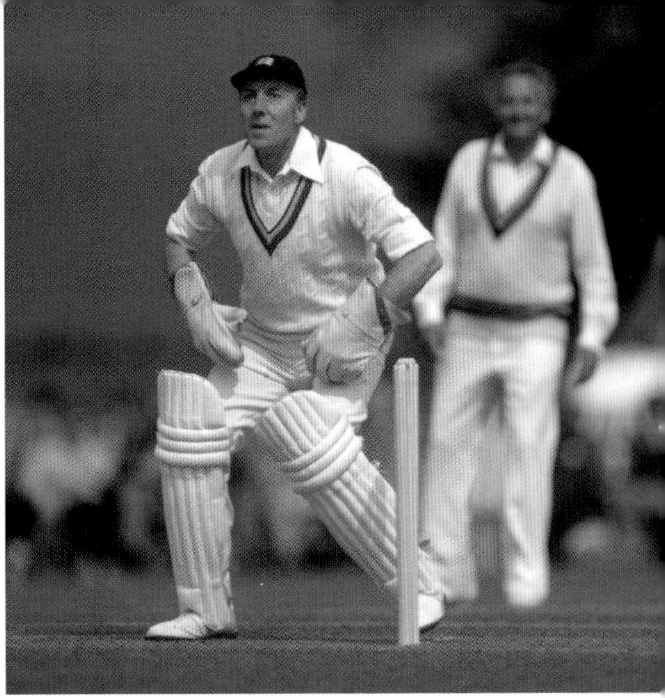

*Three years later, Murray turned out for the same team against the West Indies at Arundel, and stumped Viv Richards into the bargain.*

*With Godfrey Evans and Fred Trueman, going about their duties on behalf of the Gordon's Gin Wicketkeeper of the Month award.*

Leaving cricket apart, Murray could successfully turn his hand to most ball games.

In characteristic pose.

John and Colleen Murray in Vancouver, 2002.

Author and subject.

Murray seen at his spiritual home. For 68 years he either worked, played or simply enjoyed life at Lord's, and in July 2018 he spent his final hours watching a Middlesex victory from the committee room with a gin and tonic in hand. Just before the end he announced that it had been a perfect day.

*Golden years.*

*The happy retired cricketer, and about the best role model of how to be a sane adult in the modern world.*

with the family', the highlights of which had included 'replying to autograph letters, taking the bins out, and helping make dinner. No one at home ever made a big fuss about me,' he added, and you knew that he would have wanted it no other way. The only other thing Murray ever said on the subject of the Oval 1966 was: 'I remember old E.W. Swanton remarking that at long last England had a proper, old-fashioned stumper again – and that was high praise coming from him, because he didn't exactly throw the stuff around like confetti. I don't think he even knew I existed up till then.'[4]

Murray's Test career had always been a thing of fits and starts, and he was unlucky that there was no overseas MCC tour scheduled for the winter of 1966/67. As a result, he would have to wait nearly a year for the opportunity to build on the momentum of the Oval and at long last cement himself as England's wicketkeeper of choice. Except it didn't quite work out that way. All he could do in the meantime was to jog around his local park and eventually to go off on a brief Rest of the World tour of Barbados. In the first match he ran up 121 in three hours batting against Charlie Griffith, Wes Hall and Garry Sobers, which was more than his team-mates Tom Graveney, Basil D'Oliveira, Bill Lawry, Rohan Kanhai and Mushtaq Mohammad scored between them. Despite the heavy rain that fell on and off throughout the week, the mood was convivial in and around the Kensington Oval, Bridgetown, where the match took place. Several hundred

4 As if to prove his innings at the Oval wasn't all somehow a listless fluke, Murray went out to bat a week later for Middlesex against Sussex at Hove and top-scored with what his new admirer Swanton called '114 of the best runs imaginable'.

fans had travelled from the UK to attend the cricket Woodstock, with various local bands playing in the streets around the ground, which were thronged with brilliantly-hued outfits, a sea of heavily-churned mud underfoot where the scores of those destined not to see a ball bowled in anger reclined, casualties of drink, drugs or a combination thereof. Even in the mid-1960s, for those Britons attending an overseas sports contest it seemed that intoxication was the rule, and prolonged consciousness the exception. The tour's second and final match, also at Bridgetown, was a more subdued affair. Graveney scored an unbeaten 69 and the visitors won by six wickets. Murray never got to bat, although Swanton was again on hand to witness the 'well-graced England wicketkeeper, with the ability to make the express delivery appear to be in no hurry at all ... There is a composure and a certain lordliness about even the way he returns the ball with a majestic sweep of the arm to a nearby aide.'

It's interesting to note how often cricket's most widely regarded commentators competed to extol this same languid and apparently patrician deportment on the part of a man in fact born and raised in White City, the son of a council labourer and a factory worker. If Murray was truly a 'gifted aesthete, bring[ing] cultivation and grace to everything from the peak of his trim blue cap to his luxuriantly polished boots', as E.M. Wellings once claimed, it was as a result of sheer graft and devotion to his craft, not of any aristocratic advantage.

* * *

Despite enjoying the distinct leg-up of playing their home matches at Lord's, and of boasting a team with seven current or future Test players, Middlesex remained the perennial underachievers of English county cricket. They finished the 1966 season a lowly 13th place in the table. The side's total of 86 points was less than half that of the champions Yorkshire. Murray still sometimes captained his county when Fred Titmus was away on England duty. It has to be said that he made a workmanlike if not always Churchillian job of it, vowing to 'take each day as it comes' and generally treating his fellow professionals as adults who should be expected to simply get on with it.

The 21-year-old batsman Clive Radley was then just coming in to the Middlesex team, and later told me:

> 'John Murray, Fred Titmus and Peter Parfitt were all very much in one camp, and the rest of us in another. They'd been on tour with England together, and they had their own stories and jokes which meant nothing to the younger players. I don't mean they were aloof, just that they'd had this experience and we hadn't. But beyond all the Test caps there was a less tangible but just as impressive thing about JT: the confidence he engendered just by his aura of calmness and determination, the way he never swore or shouted whatever the circumstances. Some batsmen come back to the dressing-room after getting out and they're effing and blinding, throwing their kit around, punching holes in the wall. It's like a warzone. John would just quietly sit down, light a fag and get on with it.'

* * *

The year 1967 always seems to be wafted back to us in a haze of incense. At one moment, apparently, young people in Britain were all dutifully marching around suburbia in sensible suits and skirts, and forsaking anything more chemically potent than the occasional Disprin. At the next, they had taken to the city streets realising the oneness of all creation by gearing up in beads and kaftans, and were proffering flowers amid a psychedelic ghetto of bistros, boutiques and less easily identifiable enterprises with names like 'Head' or 'Kleptomania', while for his part the young Tom Jones was sashaying around Chelsea with a cheetah and a dolly-bird on each arm, the better to promote a new emporium called Tom Cat.

As mentioned, I experienced this heady moment in our island story from the perspective of a Victorian prep school craning out over the Sussex clifftops like a somewhat more decrepit Berghof. Whatever its other charms, it has to be said that it wasn't a spot conspicuous for its countercultural promise. My father occasionally came down to visit his old school, and he confirmed that the place remained in essence unchanged from the era of Ramsay MacDonald in Number 10 and Jack Hobbs opening the batting for Surrey. It was as though it had somehow managed to slip through a crack in the space-time continuum, to lie not so much indifferent as oblivious to the march of 1960s progress. Rottingdean may have had a lot going for it as a classically quaint English village, with an ancient flint church at one end and a black windmill at the other, but in conscience you wouldn't call either it or St Aubyns itself a mecca of venturesome youth. About a month after I first enrolled in the school my parents came down one wet Sunday afternoon to take me out to tea. I remember mentioning to my father that my English master was called Mr Kennington. 'Good Lord,' he said, genuinely shocked at the report. 'Alan Kennington had me for English here in the 1930s. He wasn't young then.'

A year or so later, I was lumbering out to keep wicket for the school's second eleven on our rather randomly mown seaside pitch that like Lord's rolled drunkenly down from north to south. In fairness that was probably its only point of resemblance to cricket's headquarters. Thistles abounded in the St Aubyns outfield, which was rumoured to have been further disfigured by a Luftwaffe bomb, and a stiff sea breeze sometimes knocked over deckchairs and sent newspapers and empty crisp packets eddying around as if the old Brighton Belle had just passed by the platform.

My skills as a wicketkeeper were limited. There were only two things I really contributed to the team when in the field. I could usually take the ball reasonably cleanly when standing back to the quicker bowlers, and, as mentioned, being broad, I presented an inviting target for the spinners to aim at. But I possessed no athletic ability whatsoever, and when it came time to bat I basically had just the one shot – a lusty heave that pretty well completed a full circle in its execution and connected with the ball on average once an innings.

The term 'role-model' barely existed back then, but the supremely elegant and remote figure of John Murray, patting the brim of his cap before nestling urbanely behind the stumps for Middlesex or England, offered an intoxicating vision of adult life as a suave, flannel-clad utopia free from the boredom and drudgery of middle age as experienced by those of my friends' parents variously described as 'doing something' in business. Despite my glaring lack of ability, or even basic aptitude, for cricket, I soon aspired to representing my country. Other than talent, I had every possible qualification. By the summer term of 1967 I could, and did, recite Murray's batting average for each of the preceding 15 seasons. I knew how many catches he took when playing for Middlesex against the 1956 Australians, and I could quote the exact phrasing of the fulsome tribute *Wisden* paid him when naming the 'impeccable wicketkeeper' one of its Five Cricketers of the Year. I think my parents began to worry only when on our summer holiday in Jersey I preferred to sit glued in front of the hotel television watching the action from Middlesex v Pakistan at a drizzly Lord's rather than hitting the local beaches.

It was worth it. Murray came in second wicket down in that match and hit the Test-strength tourists for 53 in about half an hour. I can distinctly remember one free-swinging forward stroke which was a distant and altogether more cultured relative to my own trademark yahoo, with the critical difference being that this particular blow was played against the brisk and accurate Asif Iqbal, and also that the ball sailed away to clear the Lord's pavilion rope, bringing an excited 'My word!' from the BBC commentator. Murray loved to treat fast bowlers so, and when an over or two later a frustrated Asif dropped one in short the batsman deposited him in to the leg side Tavern with the same unhurried venom.

One way or another, that exotically-scented summer looked like being a good one for the glacially cool England wicketkeeper and his hordes of impressionable young fans. After a few false starts, Murray finally seemed to be the undisputed man in possession behind the stumps. India, led by their dashing, one-eyed captain the Nawab of Pataudi – 'Tiger' to his friends – toured Britain just before the arrival of the Pakistanis. Geoff Boycott remained unbeaten on 246, scored in 573 minutes, when England closed their innings at 550/4 in the first Test at Headingley. The Indians were beaten by six wickets, but, like Barrington before him, Boycott was dropped for 'selfish batting'. Doug Insole and his panel – Peter May, Alec Bedser and Don Kenyon – evidently felt that the Yorkshireman's marathon knock failed to sufficiently advance the cause of the 'brighter cricket' they had promised the public. In other circumstances, he might have been hailed as a national hero. England won the next Test, at Lord's, too: Murray picked up six catches in the Indian first innings, which equalled the wicketkeeping world record. (They have honours boards for batting and bowling at Lord's, so why not one for exemplary fielding?) Murray then proceeded to add the Batsman of the Match award in the third Test at Edgbaston, where he top-scored with 77 out of an England total of 298. Here's what Brian Close had to say about it in his autobiography:

> 'Graveney, Barrington, Amiss, Illingworth and I were all gone, with the Indian slow bowlers still able to pitch the ball on a very responsive wicket. Against this backcloth of failure John Murray displayed the composure of an experienced batsman. He shielded Snow and Hobbs from the bowling, in two stands of 50, before he himself was caught on the

> midwicket boundary, 23 runs short of the century he so well deserved.'

England won that match, too. Murray was playing easily the best international cricket of his life, both with the bat and behind the stumps. Now was the moment to consolidate.

* * *

But he didn't.

Just ten days after beating the likes of Boycott, Barrington, Milburn, Graveney and Amiss to become England's officially recognised batsman of the hour, Murray suffered the ignominy of a pair in the first Test against Pakistan at Lord's. In mitigation it might be added that the ball generally dominated the bat in that game, where it rained heavily on each of the five days, and also that *The Times* expressed a widely held view when it reported that the England wicketkeeping had been 'very high class' and 'supremely neat' throughout, with just a single bye conceded in the one completed Pakistan innings of 354. The match itself was drawn. Nonetheless, there was a shock coming when on 6 August the team was announced for the second Test at Trent Bridge. Murray was out. So were five other members of the side that had acquitted itself well at Lord's. When I asked him about it 30 years later, Murray laughed gently.

'On the second [Friday] night it was chucking down with rain,' he remembered. 'My mate Reg Hayter had his own sports reporting agency. He knew a thing or two about cricket. "They'll never play tomorrow," he said. "Come out to dinner. I want to talk to you about publishing your biography." Well, I could take a few in those days, and so could Reg, and the end result was that we and our wives ended up in this belly-dancing club until two in the morning. I must have finally gone to bed around four o'clock. Lovely man, Reg, really knew his cricket. About five hours later I'm back at Lord's, the sun's beating down, and we get off to a prompt start in front of a full Saturday house. Halfway through the morning session Hanif Mohammad came down the track to Robin Hobbs. The ball spun out of the rough, bounced about five feet, and the batsman completely missed it. So did I. It banged off my chest and went for a bye. Hanif scored 187. Everyone was saying then how Insole wanted fresh young faces in the team, and that was probably the moment I knew my number was up. Funny game, cricket. Old Reg never came through with that book deal, either.'

When Murray told me about this I thought first how uncharacteristic it was of him to be out and about among the West End fleshpots on the second night of a Test, or for that matter at any other time, and second how trivial a possible missed take might appear when set against the copious excellence of his career as a whole. It seems curious, too, even by England Test standards, that he should have been sacked in the same short span of time in which he collected keenly-contested awards for both his batting and keeping. Of course, back then you never quite knew what to expect from the national selectors, besides their mantra of 'brighter cricket', for better or worse. Seven of the England players who started the Test series in early June 1967 would be gone again by the time it finished late in August. To call Insole the David Bowie of the international sports administration world would perhaps be to confer a flattering sense of consistency on a man who seemed to restlessly chop and change his team with each successive match in search of an elusive balance between the aesthetically pleasing and the statistically successful. Anyway, Murray was gone. He'd played 21 Tests (one of them as a specialist batsman) over the course of six years, scoring 506 runs at an average of 22, with 52 catches and three stumpings. For the record, this is a better (2.6 versus 2.4 per cent) average number of dismissals per Test than even Godfrey Evans managed. Of course statistics alone are absurd when it comes to describing a man whom you could watch as much for the pleasure of seeing the complete perfection of the wicketkeeper's art as to enjoy its material results.

For his part, Insole would go on just a year later to preside over the non-selection of the 'coloured' Basil D'Oliveira for the 1968/69 tour of South Africa, having meanwhile also been party to the decision to axe Brian Close (with a Test captaincy record of six wins and a draw) after he supposedly wasted time in a county match his side might otherwise have lost.

I admit that I wept bitter tears at the news of Murray's dismissal. The press told us that his replacement was Kent's promising 21-year-old stumper Alan Knott, whom in my anguish I thought little more than a crudely stylised burlesque act compared to my hypersmooth idol. Later I would probably have to concede that in his way Knott was a fine keeper who also made for a more nudgingly creative and generally consistent Test batsman than his England predecessor, but at the time I was appalled. There was something histrionic and more than a bit simian about the young upstart's fidgety body language, it seemed to me, and I'm ashamed to say that at the age of ten I found it somehow solaced the grief when I first read the initials 'A.P.E. Knott' printed in the newspapers.

Many years later I put it to Murray that, like me, he must have been crushed by the decision to abruptly dispense with his services just as he finally seemed to be making the England wicketkeeper's job his own, a set of circumstances that seemed to offer a toxic combination of deceit, intrigue, ambition and general duplicity of almost Shakespearean proportions. Not a bit of it. 'It was Knotty's time,' he told me evenly.

Middlesex finished the year seventh in the championship table, still by no means playing to their full potential but at least a modest upgrade on 1966. There was a curious finale to the season against Somerset at Lord's. Murray was captaining the side again, and, winning the toss, sent Middlesex out to bat. They made only 96. As a result the visitors would enjoy a first innings lead of 163, and ended up needing just 19 to win on the last morning. They were playing that match with an almost comically short Tavern-side boundary, and on the first day Somerset's Peter Robinson kept lifting the Middlesex spinners high over the fence for six nearly every other ball. Murray moved four men down on to the rope, but it was a lost cause. They just stood and stared at the ball as it sailed over their heads in to the refreshment area time after time. Robinson raced to 97, but then fell to a flying catch behind the wicket as John Price found the edge. It was a short-lived Middlesex success, because South Africa's Terry Barwell soon took up the fight. The first time Price bounced the ball at him, its next bounce occurred about ten rows back in the Tavern. It being Murray, he fought hard until virtually the end, at which point he gracefully accepted the inevitable and put himself on to bowl. His three overs of gentle swing went for 11 runs, which was pretty respectable under the circumstances, and I always remember him walking off with a broad grin, capless for once, flicking back a strand of his now noticeably thinning hair as it flapped in the breeze, with his arm around Graham Burgess's shoulder after Burgess had just hit him for the winning runs. I don't know why, it just seemed like one of those moments peculiar to English county cricket as opposed to any other professional sport.

A week later I was back at Lord's to watch a match billed as a Rothman's England XI v Rest of the World, which basically meant Garry Sobers and the cream of the West Indians with the South African Pollock brothers thrown in. There was a faintly damp, leafy, end-of-summer-holiday feel in the air. The ground was full but oddly subdued. I carried a Wimpy cheeseburger brunch to my seat. England batted first and scored 144. It wasn't much of a contest, because Graeme Pollock was knocking off the winning runs less than two hours later. After that somebody from the MCC came out to distribute medals and to tell everyone that we'd all been lucky enough to see the greatest cricketers in the world performing at the game's headquarters. It fired up the crowd, in a kind of pro forma way. For some reason, a KEEP GIBRALTAR BRITISH sign dangled down from one of the pillared boxes in the grandstand. Then someone else came on the pavilion tannoy to thank us all for coming, and to remind everyone that there was a tube strike on but that additional buses were operating – 'your journey may take longer than usual', he added, perhaps unnecessarily.

Having to get across London to Waterloo, I remember setting off with a sinking feeling a few moments later, and then abruptly pausing at the triangle of grass behind the Warner Stand – somewhere near the later failed site of the Keith Miller memorial tree – as Murray and D'Oliveira suddenly strode towards me in their flannels and blue England blazers. They split up to pass me. They had no real option in the matter, because I froze and stood there like a statue, gazing up at their faces in awe. At the very last moment, I recall piping up, 'I'm a wicketkeeper, too' – like telling Mozart you were doing a bit of this piano lark yourself – to Murray. He looked at me steadily and said, 'Jolly good.' A moment later, he added: 'Keep it up.' I don't suppose any words ever spoken to me meant more than those did. Could it be that I was now suddenly in with the greatest living Englishman, I wondered, when at length the breath returned to me, and that I had a friend and mentor who would presumably go on to graciously oversee my rapid progress from the St Aubyns seconds to full England Test honours?

Or perhaps, in retrospect, I was getting ahead of myself. After that more than 20 years passed before I spoke to Murray again.

* * *

MCC toured the West Indies that winter of 1967/68, taking Knott and Parks as wicketkeepers, with Brian Timms of Hampshire officially in reserve. Having been England's hero just a few weeks earlier, Murray now wasn't considered among the country's top three players in his position. Colin Cowdrey returned as captain, and when I later interviewed him he told me that he'd 'thought the world of JT' and 'always wanted him in or around the Test team'. That being so, I asked him what had happened when he'd sat down in the committee room at Lord's to help select the names of the 16 players to tour the Caribbean. 'Somebody has to lose out,' Cowdrey said.

Characteristically, Murray took it all in his stride, and at the age of 32 was fast coming to appreciate that there might be a life beyond cricket. A further significant milestone down this road was the birth in October 1967 of his son Nick. I once pompously suggested that taken as a whole this was a case of propitious timing, one window of opportunity closing just as another one opened up, and Murray, who rarely wasted time on metaphysical asides, just smiled gently and said that he was obviously delighted to now twice be a father, and that his family life as a whole had been a 'corker', with everything he could possibly have wanted waiting there at home for him when he came back in the evening.

'People said I was buggered about a fair bit in my career,' he added, 'but I always thought I was the luckiest bloke in the world.'

# 5.

# PLAYER

COLIN Cowdrey's formidable political skills were taxed to the hilt on the 1967/68 MCC tour of the West Indies. Here's what *Wisden* had to say of the affair:

'Chief among the unpleasant aspects were the clearly sub-standard umpiring and unruly crowds. The decision by Sang Hue against Butcher in the second Test sparked a bottle-throwing riot by the batsman's fellow Jamaicans ... There was another act of hooliganism in Guyana after the final Test, when England had won the series. There the victorious side were attacked when leaving the ground. Lock was struck on the head by a stone, and Cowdrey was long compelled to wait in the pavilion until he could safely be escorted to his

> hotel by a police guard … The difficult attitude of the [home] Board was shown again when they took the travel and hotel plans out of the hands of MCC. Some of their arrangements were by no means satisfactory.'

Despite this sorry litany, the end result was that the MCC players returned to Heathrow on 5 April 1968 bringing the Wisden Trophy with them. The Englishmen had taken the series 1-0 when Garry Sobers generously set them a target of 215 runs in 165 minutes to win the fourth Test at Trinidad. The tourists crossed the line with just three minutes to spare. Sobers, who would be playing for Nottinghamshire in 1968, was on the same plane returning to London as his recent opponents. On landing he paid a gracious tribute to the better side, and it has to be said that all in all the visitors coped well enough in Murray's absence, Knott coming in for Parks in the fourth and fifth Tests, and in *Wisden*'s view 'greatly rais[ing] the standard of wicket-keeping, which was otherwise unusually low in the series'. The one exception to the general MCC effusion was the freak boating accident that deprived Fred Titmus of four toes on his left foot. A few days later, the Middlesex spinner with the already Chaplinesque gait rang a frantically worried Murray to assure him that he would be able to play again. Sure enough, Titmus was back in action on the county circuit just two months later; initially appearing in crepe-soled shoes he took 111 wickets that summer, which was five more than he managed in 1967. He received £90 compensation (about £620 today) for his loss, or £22/10s a toe, from the MCC's insurance policy.

While the surgeons were still working on Titmus's foot, Murray was turning out for a Commonwealth XI captained by Roger Prideaux on tour of Pakistan. He did well enough in his six matches there, but the real point of his presence in the side was that it showed again the lengths to which England's sometime wicketkeeper was prepared to go for a game of competitive cricket. Richie Benaud came in to the team at Karachi in late March – his last-ever first-class appearance – and, 40 years later, told me that Murray was 'the most energetic and the most willing international cricketer in a long time. He never groused, and I always remember him coming off the field all covered in red mud after keeping beautifully all day, I might add with no help either from the pitch or the umpires, and when he got back upstairs to the dressing-room he poured himself a cup of tea and just perched there at a stool in front of his locker. It was the end of the tour, and everyone else was larking about. But John just sat there patiently concentrating on whatever he was doing at his stool, which involved stretching out a pair of inner gloves – a task he appeared completely locked in to. It was as if the rest of the room didn't exist. And then after a few more minutes he put the gloves carefully away in his bag, changed into his neat grey flannels and blazer, adjusted his tie, combed his hair, walked out with us to the bus, paused for a photo, shook the driver's hand, and then we were off. The feeling you got was of a very calm and capable English businessman of the old school who also happened to be a brilliant cricketer.'

Back at Middlesex, Peter Parfitt remembers being told he was next in line for the county captaincy when Titmus eventually stood aside. The 31-year-old all-rounder wasn't the committee's first choice for the job. 'The only reason I got the nod was because JT came back in 1968 and said in his quiet but firm way that he wanted to concentrate fully on his wicketkeeping and batting and win his England place back,' Parfitt recalls. 'So the boys in the committee room came up with a system. Fred was captain, I was his heir, and John was the wily old pro you always turned to for advice. They paid the three of us a guaranteed £10 weekly, and with bonuses you could probably take home £900 or so a season. That was big money, because up till then we got £6 a match apiece.'

Murray achieved the first part of his business plan for the year, scoring close to 1,000 runs – including an unbeaten 104 against Hampshire's all-Test bowling attack – and taking 72 dismissals, a quarter of them stumpings. But Alan Knott played in all five Tests against the touring Australians. 'I thought John was very unlucky,' says Parfitt, 'but you never once heard a breath of criticism from him, least of all about Knott. He'd read in the evening paper who was in or out of the England squad, shrug, and just get on with it. It's a cold business. And for as much as you wanted him back in the Test team, I think he knew by then that his day was up.'

Parfitt also wanted me to know that Murray was the peacemaker of the Middlesex side. 'There was a certain edge whenever we played Yorkshire. It went right back to the 1930s. They used to come down to Lord's and moan a lot about how we played all our home matches in front of the England selectors, with all that involved, and let's just say there was a certain amount of niggle going on out in the middle. Well, John put a stop to all that. "Leave it alone", he told us whenever the sledging began. He was one of those blokes who preferred to let the runs and wickets do the talking. So gradually Middlesex v Yorkshire became a civilised affair again, and I give Murray credit for ending about three generations of North–South bullshit.'

On 23 August 1968, the Cape Town-born, tan-skinned Basil D'Oliveira completed a score of 158 (after being dropped four times) while representing England against Australia in the final Test at the Oval. Later that week Doug Insole and his team met to choose the MCC party set to tour South Africa in the winter. D'Oliveira, the side's hero just days earlier, was conspicuously absent from the list. There was an immediate outcry that his exclusion was the result of some behind-the-scenes deal with the Pretoria government to protect their policy of strict racial segregation. The plot then thickened when Warwickshire's Tom Cartwright, a bowler who could bat a bit, withdrew from the tour through injury, and D'Oliveira, a batsman who could bowl a bit, was called up in his place. This was too much for South Africa's president John Vorster, who announced: 'We are not prepared to receive a team thrust upon us by people whose interests are not in the game, but to gain their political objectives.'

Like most people who actually knew him, Murray liked D'Oliveira. And, equally as characteristic, he was also wary of a streak in the Worcestershire player often described as boisterous or high-spirited, but that could also be called just 'difficult' – or mean. There was a raw determination in him, too. As Murray said, 'You'd have to kill Dolly to make him quit. He had a temper ... His attitude was always, "We'll settle this thing right now and I'm willing to go all the way to do it." A lovely mate, but also a bloody awful enemy.'

Tom Graveney once added in this context, 'Bas was always a bit of a loose cannon on tour. When we were in the West Indies in '67/'68 he was spoiling, off the park as well as on, for a fight – often for senseless fights. He got in to a scene with a younger English guy one night in a bar. I had to pry his fingers off the other bloke's neck. Generally speaking, Basil got noisier with each drink … I liked him, but he could be a handful. Always overdid the Bacchic rites.' It's possible that when Insole and his co-selectors sat down at Lord's in August 1968 they were mindful both of this fact and more pertinently of D'Oliveira's playing record in the Caribbean, which saw him score just 137 runs at an average of 23 and take three wickets at nearly 98 apiece over the course of five Tests.

As it happened, there was another mild surprise when the selectors came to release the names of the 16 players due to tour South Africa, although, unlike D'Oliveira's omission, no one asked questions about it in parliament or took to the streets in protest.

Murray was back. Or at least he was there as an understudy to Knott, who was 11 years his junior, and to provide ballast for the middle-order batting. At 37, Parks had now played his own last Test, and the likes of Bob Taylor of Derbyshire were yet to come through the ranks. Of course it was all still a moot point whether or not Murray would have the opportunity to reclaim his place, because on 17 September Vorster announced to his party congress amidst loud applause that the revised MCC squad was 'not the team of Lord's but that of the anti-apartheid movement' and as such was unwelcome. 'I have taken a stand for South Africa,' he added.

The next day, MCC's secretary Billy Griffith wrote to Murray:

> 'Dear John
> We were all extremely sad to hear Mr Vorster's announcement. No final decision regarding the tour will be made until we hear officially from the South African Cricket Association, but it would appear to be almost certain that it will be cancelled.
>
> 'In view of [this], we have today made a tentative approach to both India and Pakistan concerning the possibility of a short tour to those countries of, perhaps, 10 weeks' duration, commencing after Christmas.
>
> 'I should be grateful if you would let Mr Carr, or myself, know, if necessary by telephone, not later than 23 September, whether you would be available for such a tour, should we arrange it.'

He was, and, unfortunately, they did. As *Wisden* remarked, 'Nothing went right with England's 1968/69 plans.' The proposed Indian trip fell through, and the Pakistani one made the recent tour of the Caribbean seem like a model of civic decorum by comparison. The first two Tests in the three-Test series were drawn. The third Test took place at the National Stadium, Karachi, from 6–8 March 1969. It also ended in a draw, after a crowd of 3,000–4,000 students, apparently indignant that cricket was being played on a day marked for remembrance of those killed in recent political riots, broke down the main gate to the ground. A few moments later, the home board's president Fida Hassan, blinking the tear gas out of his eyes, arrived in the England dressing-room. 'The match is over,' he announced.

'And the tour?' asked Murray.

'And the tour.'

As a general rule, budget-conscious visits to Pakistan of that era weren't notable for their lavish public amenities or pervasive sense of customer comfort. John Snow remembers staying in an upcountry hotel where 'JT got up to go to the loo in the night and made his way to switch on the light only to realise he was walking on a bed of cockroaches.' Elsewhere on the tour, 'I recall [Murray] was very ill in bed with some stomach bug, to such an extent that our physio Bernard Thomas sat by his bed all night keeping a worried eye on him. John never once complained, though.'

Probably true, although Murray told me: 'It was a shambles, really. Riots everywhere, dodgy hotels, and some mornings you'd turn up at the ground and no one there even seemed to be particularly expecting us. We were in Sahiwal before the first Test and there was a sort of voodoo ceremony laid on for us one night on the lawn behind the hotel. A lot of blokes started banging drums, and then these dancing-girls were shimmying around in time with the music. We all clapped politely. It went on a bit. Then one of the drummers held up this white football thing and started shouting wildly at it, pushing it back and forth in front of our faces, and at that stage I realised it wasn't a football at all. It was a human skull. Next he puckered his lips up and began kissing it. Steady on, old boy, I thought, we're English. Well, we got out of there all right, but I have to say the tour as a whole was bloody frightening. We eventually flew out to Dacca and the place looked like a war zone. There were flares shooting up in the air, blokes running round the ground with guns and knives, sirens blaring. It's like the Blitz. Some of us finally fixed up a meeting at the British High Commission. Lovely chaps, very pukka, they're all in there playing bridge and drinking gin and tonic. These blokes' advice was carry on lads, keep the flag flying. They also suggested we donate a few bob as a goodwill gesture to some local charity, and Kipper [Cowdrey] said he'd do that, only when he reached in his pocket he found his wallet had been nicked somewhere between getting out of the taxi and going in the front door. It was a distance of about five yards.'

On 27 February, there was another letter from Lord's to north Wembley:

> 'Dear Mrs Murray
> I thought you would be interested to know that I have just received the following communication from Mr Les Ames, the Manager of the M.C.C. team, in Dacca:
>
> '"Rather worried what may appear in today's Press and consequent distress it could give to players' families. Amazing as it may seem, the smooth running of this Test Match depends upon the student leaders. I have interviewed them, [and] I have told them that if there is any trouble we shall withdraw. In any event, I am satisfied that the safety of the team is assured."

> 'I am sure you will be as relieved as we are to know that the situation appears to be reasonably satisfactory.'

Nine days after Billy Griffith wrote this letter, the MCC players found themselves being driven at wild speed in a convoy of camouflaged Pakistani military lorries in order to catch a hurriedly-arranged midnight plane out of Karachi. 'We were rumbling over these potholed roads,' Murray remembered, 'army blokes shouting into their walkie-talkies, guns popping off in the distance. Total bedlam. Both sets of players were being evacuated post-haste out of town. Some of them were cowering down, others were sitting there dead quiet, and amidst all this chaos there's a sort of strobe light flickering on and off from all the shooting, and I look over and see a jeep go by with Sarfraz Nawaz standing up to attention in the back. He's dressed in a three-piece suit, hair perfect, face calm. He looks like a Burton's dummy. Well, we took off and flew home via Cairo, Rome and Paris, with long delays at each stop, and when we finally got back old Tom Graveney bent down and kissed the ground. He'd had enough. So had I.' Knott had played in all three Pakistan Tests, such as they were, and *Wisden* remarked that 'Murray could act only as ballast.' It was his sixth official representative tour, and also his last.

* * *

I daydreamed my way through my last year at St Aubyns. My reading skills eclipsed my retarded comprehension of maths and science. I was a big kid. I flaunted my size and bluffed my way through confrontations. I was considered a bit odd, and with good cause. While most of my peers went home for the holidays to their family seats in the Home Counties with an ancient nanny in the attic, I flew off three times a year to a flat with a thin scrap of porridge-coloured carpet and a stone kitchen in Moscow, where my father had now been sent as the British naval attaché. It might as well have been the far side of the moon. In those days the USSR was a remote, forbidding place of the sort early map-makers used to label 'here be dragons', and the mere fact of living there got me branded 'a commie' by some of the Berkshire set. The stigma didn't particularly bother me, but I lost a fair amount of sleep worrying about the England wicketkeeper situation. It seemed cruelly unfair that Murray should have been treated in the way he was by the selectors. It's debatable whether either school or cricket did much for my long-term education, but at least Doug Insole had taught me a lesson in life. At 12, I knew that all things went chaotically bad.

Because of my father's job, I experienced the D'Oliveira Affair from the perspective of our KGB-bugged digs on Skaterniey Prospekt, about a mile downriver from the Kremlin, where I furnished my tiny bedroom with a shelf full of *Wisdens* and every photo of Murray I could find torn from the pages of the *Cricketer* or the tissue-papered airmail edition of *The Times*. It was a heady time to be behind the Iron Curtain, because just 24 hours before the England and Australia teams began their fateful Test at the Oval the Red Army invaded Czechoslovakia. I remember walking down the street one scorching hot morning and hearing an announcement rumbling over the loudspeakers attached to the tops of the lampposts.

'What are they saying?' I asked my father. He listened for a moment. 'They're telling us they're granting the request of their fraternal Czech comrades for immediate protection against imperialist subversion.'

'Is that really what's happening?' I asked.

'Not exactly,' my father replied.

As I say, heady times. Later that year I found myself sitting with half a dozen other people on the verandah of a modest suburban Moscow dacha with a bright-yellow plastic awning stretched above us, being lectured by the home's owner: the deposed Soviet hardman Nikita Khrushchev, who wore a sweat-stained white linen suit and sandals, smelled of old hay, and looked like an ex-nightclub bouncer who could still take care of himself if the need arose. At one point our host asked me what sports I liked, and I mentioned a fondness for cricket. To my surprise, he immediately launched in to a long and highly animated speech, in which the name 'D'Oliveira' was intelligible before translation. When Khrushchev eventually came up for air, his attractive female interpreter told us he'd expressed the view that 'agencies of Western deviationism', along with 'racists' and 'fools' had been responsible for Dolly's initial exclusion from the tour of South Africa, 'a country the civilised world needs like a dog needs five legs'. Judging by the way the woman blushed as she spoke these words, I imagined her boss might have added a couple of choice intensifiers to his remarks.

When Khrushchev leaned forward during this tirade, tiny pig eyes flashing, you suddenly caught a glimpse of the man who just a few years earlier had brought the world to the brink of destruction in the Cuban Missile Crisis. It was impressive and a little disconcerting that the one-time leader of 230 million Soviet citizens should know quite as much as he did about the vagaries of English cricket selection. Perhaps I should have probed him further about his personal choice for our Test wicketkeeper. I suppose it was all reflected fame of a sort, and I was regarded as even more of a pinko back at school as a result. The following June my father came down in his dress uniform to take the salute as the student body raggedly marched past him on the cricket square in our annual pre-half-term parade. Someone had pulled some strings and got Field Marshal Montgomery to do it the year before, so Dad had a hard act to follow. Earlier that morning I'd overheard some boys ask a master who was inspecting the troops that year, and without seeing me he'd answered casually: 'Nobody special.' My father would probably not have seriously dissented from this verdict. When the time came for his remarks from the reviewing stand he told us that we lived in changing times, with a man set to walk on the moon any day now, but that qualities such as civility, neatness and general self-effacement would never go out of style.

* * *

'The worst thing about full-time cricket is that a lot of it has nothing to do with cricket,' Murray once told me. 'It's about dark motorways and iffy hotels, and being nice to the sponsors and a lot of other people you'd prefer not to deal with, and doing all this six days a week – at least until 1969, when the John Player League got going, and we were suddenly working on Sundays as well. Let's just say I always loved being on the field, whether batting or keeping. The rest of it I could take or leave alone.

'You'd be dog-tired,' Murray continued, 'worried about something, usually money, it's a wet Monday morning at Dover, literally more players than spectators in the park, you trudge out there – and a funny thing happens. The game would start, and you'd suddenly remember the best part of professional cricket: cricket.'

Middlesex again underperformed that season, finishing 11th in the championship and doing only marginally better in the new Sunday league. Murray distinguished himself with 67 dismissals and a batting average of just under 30. In a career that had begun in 1952, he had now scored over 14,000 first-class runs, with 15 centuries. These were not the figures of a dilettante. Alan Knott ended the summer of 1969 with a dozen fewer dismissal and a batting average ten points lower than that of his England predecessor. Knott played in all six of the year's Tests against the West Indies and New Zealand.

Murray described the onset of the 1970s to me as a 'bloody awful winter' with the consolation of a month spent in Jamaica with an International Cavaliers team under Colin Cowdrey. 'And we had a high old time, sunbathing, playing a bit of cricket, and other things besides,' he said. 'For once our wives came out on tour, and there was a big do one night at the hotel, flaming torches, rum punches, steel band, the lot. Well, Godfrey Evans was there. He was about 50 then, still had the moves, but you could see him struggling a bit in the last session. "You're playing tomorrow, son," he'd tell me as he lumbered back at the close. You'd think he was dead on his feet. But there he was at the party a couple of hours later, and he's going some, my word, and out of the corner of my eye I see him chug over to Ted Dexter's lovely model wife Susie, who's wearing a short skirt, and promptly sling her over his shoulder and start to shake her around like a sack of spuds. Maybe it's some sort of new dance move I'm not familiar with, but even so Susie doesn't look too thrilled about it, and for that matter neither does Ted, and in the end a couple of us formed an extraction team and got Godders safely upstairs to bed. Amazing man. Your first thought when you saw him plod off at the end of the day was that he'd completely had it – and then he'd bounce back again first thing in the morning like one of those punching bags that keep snapping to attention no matter how hard you hit it, light on his feet, twinkle in his eye, wide grin, and keeping like he was 21 again. Never saw anyone to touch him on or off the field.' Evans in full sail was certainly one of the great sights of post-war English cricket. I once asked him about Murray. 'Best wicketkeeper of his generation,' he said immediately. 'Should have come in to the Test side right after me and stayed there about ten years,' he added.

I left St Aubyns that same winter. Most of the staff there seemed able to contain their regret. The school magazine for my last summer term – the season of bed-ins and Woodstock and other exotic late-1960s artefacts inappropriate here in Rottingdean – isn't very laudatory:

> 'On a bumpy pitch Sandford did his best behind the stumps, but repeatedly found the bounce of the ball too pronounced for him.'

I see we lost that particular single-innings encounter by 116 runs. And later in the same season:

> 'Owing to absences, Sandford was promoted to the senior eleven, but was unfortunately quite outfoxed.'

Some people have dreams in which they're running at top speed, but it's as though they're wading through glue. That was me as I vainly tried to dive after an errant delivery down the leg side. 'You might as well ask Hadrian's Wall to field the ball,' our games master observed. 'At least it wouldn't let through as many byes as Sandford does,' one of my team-mates added unhelpfully. Our head of English Alan Kennington had been a moderately successful novelist in the 1940s (they filmed his book *The Night Has Eyes*, with James Mason in the lead), and he showed a literary turn of mind when he said of my wicketkeeping in his end-of-term report that I reminded him of Samuel Taylor Coleridge: 'Like the Ancient Mariner, he stoppeth one of three,' he wrote.

Probably the most impressive statistic I can glean from the tattered grey-cloth scorebook in front of me is the number of opposing batsmen who were either caught behind or stumped in our eight matches that 1969 season. None. Tom Graveney once told me that he'd been playing against Murray in a county match at around this same time, and the Middlesex fielding as a whole had been impressively sharp, but that 'John took the whole thing up a notch when I lifted my heel just a fraction after missing a ball from Titmus, and in that same split-second, faster than you could possibly have had the thought, Murray whipped the bails off.' If you were playing against my team, you could have walked halfway down the pitch, stopped to do a leisurely bit of gardening, and then strolled back again while whistling most of the chorus of *Hello, Dolly*, and still not been out. When I changed schools that winter my pin-ups of John Murray came with me.

* * *

'Around 1970 it dawned on me that my England days were probably over,' Murray once said. He was rising 35, and already in his 19th season as a professional cricketer. Knott had played in the last 16 consecutive Tests, and looked like he might hang around. As it happened, neither wicketkeeper would add to his total of international caps in the summer of 1970. The South Africans had been due to visit, but the tour was cancelled in the wake of the D'Oliveira saga, and a Rest of the World side under Garry Sobers hurriedly stepped in. *Wisden* called them 'one of the strongest teams ever to take the field' and thought only Australia in 1921 and 1948 could have rivalled them. The visitors won a well-subscribed five-match series with England 4-1. Neither set of players was pleased when the authorities later ruled that these were not official Tests, and that they should thus be erased from the record books. D'Oliveira himself scored 308 runs in just seven innings and later remarked: 'If batting against people like McKenzie, Procter, Sobers and Gibbs in front of a full house over five days doesn't qualify as a top-class match that's just deranged. It was the hardest series I ever played in.' Murray at least got on to the field against the Rest as a member of T.N. Pearce's side in late season at Scarborough. The tourists ran up a total of 574 runs in their two innings, with a single bye. Set 346 to win on the last day, Murray was sent in first to liven things up with Geoff Boycott, and immediately got in to the spirit of it with a skimming four off his first ball – a thunderous lofted straight drive against the heavy roller, disturbing some pigeons by their proximity to its flight. After that he made 19 in another couple of overs, but fell throwing the bat against the young Indian seamer Saeed Hatteea. The match was drawn.

Murray confirmed that the early 1970s as a whole 'weren't the greatest time in English cricket history – or at least they weren't at Middlesex', he added, with a soft chuckle. The glamour team of the county circuit would finish the first season of the new decade competing with Gloucestershire to prop up the championship table. Apart from a general absence of truly proficient batting, bowling or fielding, there was a simmering debate about the side's captaincy. 'Half our time was spent talking about it,' a then-young Middlesex player told me, still sounding mildly exasperated about the fact nearly 50 years later.

'It was a total soap-opera. Fred [Titmus] had been having personal troubles at home, and wasn't in a fit state to lead an old lady across the street, let alone a professional sports team. So Parfitt took over. A nice bloke, I wouldn't call him the greatest strategic thinker in cricket history. Some people were muttering that Eric Russell or even Clive Radley should get the job. The amateur tradition still ran deep at Lord's in those days, so one or two others were banging on about Mike Brearley. Brearley wasn't even in the side full-time in 1970, but we all knew him. He did speak beautifully, Mike, lovely manners, soft-voiced, very refined, didn't like to hear anyone swearing around him. Fucking hell, I said, it's not the fucking Girl Guides is it? Anyway, not a happy place, our dressing-room, with a constant smell of stale fag smoke and general doom and gloom in the air. And in the midst of all this flak Murray was the seasoned old sergeant major. Except he didn't shout. He'd seen it all. He just turned up, shut his ego down and walked out there day after day, kept wicket beautifully, walked back again, always composed, very civil, not into the backstabbing or politics, had a quiet word now and then, kept smiling. He was everyone's favourite uncle.' Neat, trim and serenely laid-back without ever being shy about offering an opinion, Murray by all accounts exuded what amounted to an almost zen-like calm amidst the internecine squabbling and tantrums of the typical Middlesex team meeting, where the prevailing dynamics would have caused comment among the homicidally feuding Garnett family of TV's *Till Death Us Do Part*.

'In those days one of the best fixtures was always the Whitsun game between Middlesex and Sussex at Lord's,' Murray told me. 'Somehow the sun usually shone, there was a good turnout, and the Sussex lads didn't say no to a pint or two afterwards.' Middlesex went in to bat first in the match played in May 1970, and Murray scored 66 in just over an hour at the crease. 'I saw off the likes of Snow, Buss and Greig,' he remembered, 'and after that lot, old Don Bates came on from the Nursery End. Now, I liked Don. A very steady bloke. But let's face it, he was knocking 40 by then, and he was about as quick as my granny. So I fancied giving it a bit of wallop. I'd already hit him for a four through midwicket, and got an easy couple past square leg from his attempt at a bouncer. I knew it was time for the swinging yorker.

'Instead, I got a slow full-toss which seemed to float down like a big red ball of feathers,' Murray continued. 'You could have done *The Times* crossword puzzle while it was in the air. After a bit I stepped out to cart it somewhere over the North Gate. But instead of doing that I got a top edge and the ball went straight back up in the air whence it came and dropped down again into Don's hands, which he was holding out in front of him like he was praying. You never saw a more surprised-looking bowler. Tony Greig was laughing so hard he had to stuff a handkerchief in his mouth as I walked past him on the way back to the pavilion. Very droll lot, the Sussex boys were in those days.'

The record books confirm most of this, although of the Sussex second innings, a day later, they also note: 'D.L. Bates c sub, b Murray 20.' The match was drifting to a draw by then, and the Middlesex keeper turned his arm over with the highly creditable figures of 3.4-0-7-1. I asked Murray about it. 'I could do straight up-and-down medium-paced stuff if I needed to,' he said. 'Nothing rapid, mind you. Bates was an old Brighton FC inside-forward and he had dodgy knees. He was a bit slow coming out to my quicker one, such as it was, and spooned it straight to mid-on.

'Shortly afterwards I found myself bowling to John Snow. There was nothing wrong with his knees, and he put my first ball to him about six rows back in the grandstand.'

* * *

Murray slipped gracefully in to professional old age, still taking catches, scoring runs, and favouring the junior Middlesex players with a few choice words of wisdom accumulated over the course of 20 years on the county circuit.

'John's pep talks weren't exactly pearls from Churchill,' the county's opener Mike Smith once told me. 'You didn't get fight-them-on-the-beaches as much as you did, "Slow it down, mate," or "She's popping – drop one in short." Stuff like that he could see from behind the stumps. Ken Barrington always got a hearty "Morning, Colonel" when he came out to bat. John was never one of those guys who burn with hatred for the opposition. He wanted to winkle them out, sure, but he did it the old-fashioned way, by graft, not with a lot of quasi-science or mumbo-jumbo about getting in the other bloke's head.'

Murray himself told me that for all of cricket's new fixation in the 1970s with the mental aspects of the game, back in the dressing-room it was still always the same conversation. The fastidious wicketkeeper was as a rule not one for vulgarity, but he permitted himself an exception in this case. 'Hit them as hard as you fucking can,' he summarised. 'If you asked most English county cricketers what they loved about the game, none of them would tell you it was the subtle psychology of it.' While continuing to play six or seven days a week from late April to early September, Murray was now spending his off-season travelling around the country for the old Warwickshire wicketkeeper-turned-sports promoter Derrick Robins. 'The basic idea was that I went out and sold squash courts for him. Or I tried to. I was very lucky. "Take your time, and when you retire we'll make it a full-time job," Robins told me.' Though he made no complaint about his salary at Middlesex, Murray grumbled gently over the fact that his county blazer was now beginning to show signs of wear and tear after some 20 years' use, and the committee told him that if he wanted a new one he would have to buy it out of his own pocket.

* * *

Cancer imposes innumerable indignities on its victims. In addition to possible death, the disease, its complications and its treatment also force patients through the most inhumane gauntlet of our public health system. When you're not giving a blood sample, you're likely hooked up to a drip full of toxins, or losing your hair, or being sick, or generally relinquishing the will to live as you sit alone patiently awaiting your turn in a dusty hospital corridor in the Channel Islands, 5,000 miles from your childhood home and family in the American north-west, while your spouse is away serving his country on a naval guided-missile destroyer and your teenaged son, a mixed blessing at the best of times, is similarly off the scene at boarding school.

I mention this only because it sketches out some of our family circumstances in the early 1970s, and in particular what happened to my mother after we moved back from Cold War Moscow to the less racy surroundings of a granite-fronted, two-bedroom rental home in semi-rural Jersey. Disillusionment quickly set in. It was a small, damp house which seemed to be wrapped in permanent silence, and dark enough so that even in summer the hallway light was left switched on in the afternoon. My mother never complained. The two of us were alone in the place one evening during the school holiday and I made both our dinners, a junk-food collation in my case, toast and water in hers. My mother ate off a tray in her bed. After a few minutes she quietly said, 'I'm sorry', which at the time I assumed was just for the meal, but I now realise was probably an expression of broader regret. To my eternal shame I silently accepted the apology, which seemed to me no more than was my due. As soon as I decently could I retired to my little den in the attic with a collapsed two-seater sofa and the latest magazine pictures of Murray on the wall. I loved to read and sleep. I loved to illicitly smoke unfiltered Capstan cigarettes that I pilfered from my father's navy-issue, metallic-grey tins and watch sport on my bubble-screen portable TV. The room was my all-purpose domain.

My new school was out near Oxford, and one of its less dreary features was the expansive games field with its timbered pavilion, which may have lacked a bracing tang of sea air but otherwise was all immeasurably better than St Aubyns. I later discovered that Ted Dexter had learned to play there, and he described the place this way in his autobiography: 'The facilities [were] among the finest in the country – a colossal stretch of flat grassland, nigh on half a mile and dead straight out from the school.'

Of course, that was the first eleven playing area he was writing about. You would have to walk for most of that half a mile, then down a dip between two clumps of trees and in to a small valley pitted and scarred like a grenade range in order to find the outlying spot where I squatted behind the stumps. I also later came to learn that the school's magisterially remote and forbidding headmaster, a gown-clad demigod somehow appropriately named Mr Silk, was none other than the man who led John Murray and the other MCC players on their 1960/61 tour of New Zealand, and who had appeared at the breakfast table there one morning with what Murray called 'the biggest black eye you ever saw', although clearly there must have been some innocent explanation for this. Mr Silk was a morally austere figure with, we knew, impressive literary connections, including a close latter-day friendship with Siegfried Sassoon. He could never have done anything unseemly. I only once got up the nerve to ask him about Murray, and he looked at me steadily before answering in his deep, precise voice: 'A lovely wicketkeeper.' That made it official, then.

An MCC team under Ray Illingworth toured Australia that winter of 1970/71. In all there were seven Tests, one of them abandoned without a ball bowled, which the visitors won 2-0, as well as the first one-day international in cricket history, the Australians easing home by five wickets. Boycott had his most prolific series with 657 runs at 93.85, and Snow's 31 scalps were the most by an English bowler in Australia since Bodyline days. Alan Knott kept in all the Tests, with Bob Taylor as his understudy. In retrospect it wasn't only a successful tour in its own right, but also a vital evolutionary stage, the primordial soup from which all the game's modern ODI and other speed formats would emerge. Clearly, there was no going back now for a player who had come of age during the Len Hutton era.

Murray did, however, appear in an International XI under Micky Stewart's captaincy on tour of Pakistan in early 1971, marking his third visit to the country in as many years. These were not especially settled times on the subcontinent as a whole. Recent cataclysmic floods in East Pakistan had claimed 200,000 lives and destroyed up to 12 million homes, and were followed in turn by the breakdown first of parliamentary government and then of all domestic law and order. The chaos eventually led to the events that brought about Pakistan's dismemberment in

December 1971. A simultaneous 13-day cross-border dispute with India may have caused as many as three million civilian deaths. India and its Soviet ally jointly declared the outcome of the war, and the emergence of Bangladesh from the ruins of East Pakistan, to be a triumph for socialist and democratic principles.

This was the backdrop to the third and final match played by the international team in Pakistan, against a strong Board of Control side at Lahore. The short goodwill visit had not been entirely free of incident up until then. In fact the tourists' previous match at Dacca had come to an abrupt end shortly after Murray, who was batting at the time, 'happened to notice that the Pakistani lad who was fielding down at long leg edged up to the slips and muttered to them, "There will be trouble", about a split-second before there was a flash of light and someone set the main grandstand on fire. The next thing I knew we were back in the middle of an army escort again, tearing down a dark road to the airport, something of a tradition for me in those parts, as guns rang out to the left and right of us. In the midst of all this, Micky Stewart cupped his mouth to my ear and said, "Another day in paradise then, JT."' The two teams at least got through the drawn match at Lahore, constantly interrupted by pitch invasions and crowd disturbances as it was. Murray top-scored with 52 out of the international side's innings of 175/9 declared, and Pakistan gave a first ever outing to a local 18-year-old all-rounder named Imran Khan.

When I asked him about it Murray couldn't even remember Imran's performance in the match, but it was enough for 77-year-old Wing Commander Bill Shakespeare, the chairman of Worcestershire, and his county secretary Joe Lister, both of whom were accompanying the tour, to offer the teenager a one-year contract at £22/10s a week, the modest origins of one of the great careers in modern professional cricket that led 47 years later to his election as his country's prime minister.

* * *

A decade after making his first-class debut, and hot off lecturing in philosophy at Newcastle University, 29-year-old Mike Brearley finally took over the troubled Middlesex captaincy in 1971. It was an eminently civilised and somehow peculiarly English sort of revolution. 'You were supposed to know your place,' Brearley recalled of the typical county dressing-room as he'd experienced it in the early 1960s. 'You kept quiet, and you learned the game by watching other people. If you voiced an idea, they would think, "Has he paid his dues? No. Well, what's he speaking for?"' All this was now set to change, the new captain announced. Middlesex would be playing 'purposeful cricket', Brearley further informed the press, and 'every player, however junior, will be heard'.

Murray told me that he had had mixed feelings about it all. When the captain asked him – but *only* when he asked him – he weighed in with his opinion on such matters as batting tactics or field placings. It wasn't that the cheerfully unintellectual wicketkeeper sulked his way through the highbrow Brearley era. Rather, 'I just got on with it – the last thing Mike needed was me rabbiting away behind the stumps. My thinking was, keep your trap shut and play your heart out for the team. Let's face it, we needed a change. We hadn't won the title since 1949.'

Fred Titmus, who actually appeared in that championship-winning season, added: 'During the whole Brearley era, there was no trace of bolshiness or ego about JT, just a superb professional ... The situation brought out the finest in him.'

Yet to acquire the all-knowing, Yoda-like status he later enjoyed as captain of Middlesex and England, Brearley at least led his county to a respectable sixth place in the 1971 championship table. I once asked him if he'd felt adequately supported by his senior players, and he told me there had been 'no problems'. It has to be said that Murray's own season wasn't particularly crowned by statistical success: 586 first-class runs at an average of 17, along with a total of 46 dismissals, which was 17 fewer than Alan Knott.

What the figures don't show is the sheer polish Murray still brought to the job, employing what his new admirer E.W. Swanton called a 'basically sound, two-fisted method' that also allowed for 'glorious improvisation that saw him glide around, gathering throws from the field one-handed' and make catches 'incredibly wide' of the line of the stumps. Lyn Wellings agreed that Murray was 'essentially orthodox, but with the instinct and reflexes that let him pull off the really dramatic stumping or the impossible flying catch ... Like all the best wicketkeepers, he was correct before he was clever.' This was a fundamental truth about every great sportsman, Wellings added.

Godfrey Evans was managing a pub in Petersfield in the early 1970s – surely the definitive case of the poacher-turned-gamekeeper – and once took the afternoon off to watch Hampshire play Middlesex nearby. He told me that the one thing he remembered of an otherwise mediocre game was the way Murray kept wicket. 'Maybe no one else would have cared, or even noticed, but I saw how he made a mark behind the off stump and then planted his left foot there, which meant he could ride with the ball to his left – over the bails – without moving his feet. What that means is more catches and stumpings, and less byes. It sounds simple, but you'd be surprised how many keepers half-arse about, not keeping still, flopping around like a bloody fish on a deck. What you really want to do is to make something difficult look easy, not the other way round.

'No one in modern cricket had better technique than Murray,' Evans continued. 'No one had more class or style, or looked better in flannels. They fitted him as if they were a Savile Row suit.' People always seem to describe Murray as suave and elegant, and of course he was, but Evans saw other qualities as well. 'John was hardworking, dedicated and always professional,' he said. 'He was an old-fashioned stumper – more than me in some ways – who adapted to the times. Let's say he was the best of the ancient and the best of the modern.' Evans concluded by reinforcing the message he must have told me a dozen times about his England successor. 'Murray was a winner.'

* * *

As usual, I sent off a luridly hand-drawn card to Murray, addressed care of Lord's, in time for his birthday on 1 April 1972. These kitschy annual offerings took me hours to produce, with baroque, cricket-themed graphics, primary colours, and what I fancied to be parchment-style lettering. Mr Kennington wrote in my report one spring term that in contrast to my official schoolwork I'd 'burned like a candle through life's long night' to produce that year's psychedelic Murray tribute, and indeed there was something more than a little excessive – perhaps manic – to the whole enterprise. The recipient of all this industry sometimes wrote back with a little card saying 'Many thanks' or 'Best wishes' above his signature, which I displayed on my bedroom wall like a religious text. I still have most of them today. I'm sure Murray himself instantly and very rightly dismissed the whole correspondence from his mind, although about 30 years later he assured me he still remembered it.

Later that same week in April, I came home on my bicycle one Friday evening and found my father sitting alone in our front room. He told me calmly that my mother had died that morning in hospital. The two of us silently ate dinner together, and then we shook hands and I went to bed. I was 15 and from that day on I found I was no longer quite as sick with worry for John Murray every time I watched him go out to bat, nor as proud to my core at each elegantly-wrought move he made behind the stumps. It was nothing personal about JT. I just wanted to be alone in my all-pervasive world of gloom.

Murray himself survived in my absence quite well. The Australians were touring again in the summer of 1972. They beat England at Lord's in the second Test but met their match against Middlesex on the same ground a few days later. It rained a lot and evidently the light was atrocious. Murray didn't bat in the Middlesex first innings, and when he went out in the second he immediately got a glancing blow on his head from the Australian fast bowler. Clive Radley was at the other end, and he recalled that it was hard going – 'every other ball was in the ribs'. But neither batsman appealed against the light, and

Murray fought his way to 68. In the end the Aussies scraped home, but they knew they'd been in a fight. Murray didn't just sit astride his bat, either, consistently hooking and pulling the quicks down to the Tavern boundary, which he could hardly have seen in the gloom. That began a run of scores for him of 40, 44, 41, 11, 84, 12, 50 and 25 not out, which would seem to refute the idea that he was past it, or had never had it in the first place, as a batsman. He averaged around 26 that wet season, which put him on a par with the likes of Zaheer Abbas at Gloucestershire or Garry Sobers at Nottinghamshire, and well above Sobers's young county team-mate Derek Randall.

Murray saw in 1973 as part of a strong Derrick Robins team in South Africa, the first to tour there since the country's isolation. Robbins gave the stock response when asked about apartheid: 'I don't want to talk about politics, but I'll say this – we're a group of English cricketers on a private tour, here to play anyone our hosts want us to play against.' Murray later told me in his characteristically modest and fair-minded way both that he'd been surprised to find himself back among a Test-level team anywhere in the world, let alone South Africa, and also that he'd confirmed beforehand that his side's opponents would be picked strictly on merit, not their skin colour. He captained the Robins eleven when they came to play what amounted to a full-scale ODI in early February at the Wanderers ground in Johannesburg. South Africa won in the last over.

Murray was back for his 22nd season at Middlesex later that spring of 1973. The county slumped to 13th in the championship table, and went out to Tony Greig's Sussex in both the major limited-over competitions. Chasing 306 to win on the last day away to Surrey in late August, Middlesex were in some bother at 107/5. Murray walked out to bat in what seemed like a lost cause. In the next hour 80 more came for the sixth wicket, mostly runs truly made off a lively attack and fielding that was generally regarded as the best of any team on the circuit. The visitors' 38-year-old wicketkeeper pulled one ball, from outside the off stump, for six to square leg, and repeatedly sent Geoff Arnold whistling over midwicket to the gasometer boundary. Murray eventually made 124, which was only eight fewer than his ten team-mates did between them. He perished going for another short-arm smash to the ropes, and Surrey won by 29 runs.

Peter Parfitt was then winding down his long career, and remembers that Murray was as good as ever as he approached his own 40th birthday, with the added bonus that 'if he ever did somehow miss a chance, he knew enough just to dust himself off and get on with it – you'd never catch him sprawled on the deck, or rolling about pretending to be dead like some million-quid footballer'. This same pragmatic approach to his duties typified Murray's private life. Parfitt adds that in the course of 60 years' friendship, 'I can't remember John ever throwing a fit or expressing dislike for anyone.' Another senior Middlesex player says that Murray 'wasn't one to dwell on what you might call the deeper verities of life. He was a cheerful, unpretentious pro – bought you a beer at the close of play and then disappeared back to his family. His ambitions in those days? Very simple, I should think. He wanted to play his absolute best for Middlesex, and put aside a little extra for his retirement.'

* * *

'There was lightness deep within J.T. Murray. There was civility and respect and appreciation, too, and you saw it in him both on and off the park. He obviously believed in giving it 100 per cent all day, every day, when he was in the middle. But he also believed it when he told the younger players that their life after cricket would be more important than their life during cricket, and that what really mattered was family. I admired that about him. He never wanted any fame, didn't care who knew him other than what they knew about him as a cricketer. If you got to know John a bit you knew he was a very, very steady guy.

'Really, he was the sort of man who, if something happened to you and you had to give your kids to somebody, you'd give them to him.'

Fred Titmus told me this in 2002. It sums up a widely held view Murray's fellow cricketers had of him as the consummate professional who also had a life beyond the boundary. At the end of 1973, in a letter to Derrick Robins, Murray wrote, 'I think I've got two seasons left – I'm getting tired of the routine of being away from my family so much … it's time I step out.' He later added that he'd thought long and hard about his future during another 'bloody awful' winter in which periodic strikes plunged the country into total darkness and people sat in unheated rooms, their televisions shut down, reading flimsily printed newspapers by candlelight. There may have been no village in the Carpathians quite as primitive as London in the hangover years following the Swinging Sixties. In time Murray escaped by going back on tour with Robins's side in South Africa. He caught everything that came his way there, finishing with a batting average of 30. But he admitted he was tired, too, and Roger Tolchard stood in for two of the five de facto Tests. It was clear Murray's days as a full-time cricketer were numbered.

'I don't care how knackered John gets,' Robins told Fred Titmus. 'I don't care how old he is. I love him and I hate to see him go.'

* * *

In 1974, Mike Brearley led Middlesex back to the slopes of respectability with a sixth-place finish in the championship. It also ended up being a fair year for Murray, who turned 39 just before the season began. He added another 51 first-class dismissals, which was on a par with the likes of Alan Knott and Bob Taylor, although his total of 15 stumpings was more than twice what they managed between them. He had his moments with the bat, too. In early June, Murray scored 43 and an unbeaten 82 on a green wicket at Lord's against a Lancashire attack led by England's Peter Lever and Ken Shuttleworth. Later in the summer he found himself captaining T.N. Pearce's side against the touring Pakistanis at Scarborough, and rose to the occasion by scoring 70 not out in his one call at the crease. There were no byes in either Pakistan innings. More than the figures, though, Murray still had the old panache. It was the brisk march with which he took the field – 'looking as crisp and fresh as the star of a Persil commercial', the *Cricketer* wrote – and the way he first settled and then sprang up from behind the stumps, seeming both fast and completely unhurried in his taking of the ball, and the time-honoured cap-tapping ritual between deliveries, and a half-dozen other little quirks and mannerisms that endured right to the end, that seemed to place him in a more refined cricketing past when wicketkeepers generally refrained from cavorting around like circus acrobats: all that was what made him a curiosity and a star. In press reports, Murray never merely took a catch or made a stumping: he 'leapt with an elastic, feline grace', or 'swept his hands forward like the mechanism of a finely tuned Swiss watch'. But he was now vulnerable to the turning ball when batting, and was a martyr to the googly. Once late that season, at Hove, facing Sussex's Paul Phillipson, a player 17 years his junior, the Middlesex veteran wafted one well wide of his leg stump straight back in to the grateful hands of Alan Mansell, a wicketkeeper born the year Murray made his county debut. According to the *Argus*, 'he departed with a warm nod of appreciation to the fielder'. 'During the last month of that season I was bloody tired,' Murray later admitted. 'No excuses. I just wasn't finding the middle of the bat like I used to.'

'So this is how it ends,' one critic wrote of him after the match at Hove, 'not with a bang, but with a thin edge behind.'

In fact it didn't quite end there. Middlesex awarded Murray a rare second benefit season in 1975, and he quietly announced that he would step down at the end of it. At 40 he was still the neat and trim figure of his youth, though his hair was now vanishing, and for those who cared to look closely there were faint grooves, or worry-lines, etched into either cheek. It wasn't a young god the fans saw now, but an old pro, going through it all one last time. Playing against Essex at a dark Lord's in late May, Murray top-scored with an unbeaten 70 in the first innings and an unbeaten 88 in the second. He later told me that he felt he was batting as well as he ever had, at least against pace. When it came to spin he adjusted his stance, showing the bowler a bit more of his chest than the coaching manual might have liked, and if all else failed trusted brute force to get him through. He scored a lot of runs through midwicket. Murray's revised approach to batting, coupled with a shrewd appreciation of the quick single, did for him more or less what the devil did for Robert Johnson down at the crossroads. He finished that season with an average of 25, well above the likes of his England successors Taylor and Tolchard, to whom he also differed in actively relishing the short-pitched delivery. When John Lever tried bouncing him early on in the first innings of the Essex match, Murray responded with a full, long-armed swing of the bat in the direction of the Tavern stand. There was a fielder down there, and the ball flew about nine feet above his head and cracked off the drum-tight metal shutters of a kebab stall that promptly shot it back again like a trampoline. Lever stood there with his hands on his hips for a moment or two. A season's average of around 25 probably doesn't sound that much, but there was an authority about Murray's batting when he got going that suggested the stylish savagery of a Dexter or even a Botham. He rarely actually scored 25, of course, preferring either to depart early or instead to give it the big stick for one of those brutal late-middle-order cameos that turned the screw on the tiring bowlers.

Nor could it be concluded on the evidence of 1975 that Murray's standards had noticeably slipped in his specialist position. In fact he was 'just finding his feet' behind the stumps, he told his friend John Thicknesse of the London *Evening Standard*. Shortly before lunch at Lord's on Saturday 31 May,

Surrey's Dudley Owen-Thomas edged Tim Lamb into Murray's gloves to apparently become the wicketkeeper's 1,496th career victim, thus beating Bert Strudwick's world record set back in the 1920s. Legend insists that Fred Titmus, standing at slip, had promptly whipped out a pocket camera to capture the moment, though this detail has proved difficult to corroborate.[5]

By then I was notionally reading history at Cambridge, where in general life was less a matter of *Brideshead*-like spangled palisades than it was of self-imposed squalor and boredom. Having single-handedly put several points on United Spirits stock during that summer term of 1975, I was in London for a couple of nights before going off to work in a meat-packing plant in Gibraltar over the long vacation. On a whim I wandered in to a nearly-deserted Lord's one morning. The Middlesex players were just walking out on the field to start their match with Gloucestershire, who oddly enough included my new college friend Alastair Hignell in their ranks. As far as I remember, I was sporting a patched-denim ensemble and a Chairman Mao cap rakishly pushed back on my head. The last time I'd seen Murray up close I'd been wearing a crested school blazer. It somehow seemed faintly ludicrous for me even to be there. I thought my hero-worshipping days were long over, at least as

5 Cricket record-keeping was a bit more haphazard then than it is now, and in some versions Strudwick's record actually fell in Middlesex's next match, at Southampton, or even three weeks later at Old Trafford. Murray himself always preferred to go for the original date, if only because of its comic potential. As he put it: 'Mr Dudley Owen-Thomas of KCS Wimbledon and Cambridge University, bowled by the Honourable Timothy Lamb of Shrewsbury School and Oxford University, caught by John Murray of St John's Church of England School, Notting Hill, and Titmus always asked: "Who's the odd man out?"'

far as cricket went. When the match started it was so quiet you could hear Murray's hands close round the ball with a snap of the gauntlets. Then, gradually, an odd thing happened. I was a supposedly jaded university morale problem and JCR drinking champion, but as I watched the familiar smooth-moving figure behind the stumps the dormant ten-year-old in me woke with a start. It was like it was 1967 again. There, just about 40 yards away, with no one in between us, that was *him*. He was *right there*. Murray quickly caught four of the first five Gloucester batsmen. Somehow I could see and hear things now I'd missed in the past: Brearley cajoling, Titmus gabbing away, Murray one of the few grown men who could make the act of squatting seem positively dignified, perfectly still, poised, the picture of relaxation and concentration, never shouting or emoting. It rained after tea and Middlesex were out for 59.

I changed my plans and came back the next morning to watch the follow-on. Murray went in before lunch and hit 67 in classic style, banging anything short over the midwicket fence. He kept batting under a grey sky, literally like November – snow had stopped play in a county match at Buxton just a couple of days earlier – until, true to form, the Gloucester leg-spinner Sadiq trapped him with what looked suspiciously like a googly. I walked quickly round to the side of Q stand and stood there clapping in my black Mao cap as Murray strode towards me. Later I watched him signing pictures and scorecards for a small scrum of schoolboys at the back of the pavilion. He gave each of them his familiar, looping autograph and smiled broadly for a couple of amateur snapshots. I knew Murray wouldn't want to be bothered by a long-haired yob who smelled of tequila, so

I didn't go over and tell him how he'd made me feel for the last day or two. After a while I watched him stroll off into the dusk, whistling to himself as he did so.

* * *

John Murray played his last first-class match in September 1975, away to Leicestershire, on the same ground and against the same opponents he'd faced on his debut 23 years earlier. I once mentioned this coincidence to him, and he very typically asked, 'How did Middlesex do that season?' Only 11th place in the table, I told him, although they also managed to get to the Gillette Cup Final, where they lost to Lancashire, meaning that Murray at least went out of top-flight cricket in front of a full house at Lord's. They applauded him all the way to the wicket. During his career as a whole, he'd taken 1,527 dismissals, of which 259 were stumpings, three times claiming eight victims in an innings. He also scored 18,872 runs, with 16 centuries, at an average of nearly 24. As a bowler, his 55 overs brought him six wickets at 40 apiece. Of course, you might as well judge him on statistics as review a book by counting the number of words in it. Amidst all the plaudits, Murray had his regrets, too: Middlesex had failed to win a trophy of any sort during his long tenure, and for one reason or another he'd appeared in just a fifth of the 105 Tests England played between June 1959, when Godfrey Evans left the scene, and June 1969, the point at which Evans believed his county successor Alan Knott was fully ready for international duty. Murray never publicly complained, thinking himself fantastically lucky to have played as long and as happily as he did, although in a quiet moment years later he remembered how his friend Reg Hayter had again approached him about publishing his biography in 1975, and how this might have dealt with some of his frustrations at the hands of Doug Insole and the England selectors.

Hayter wanted to call his book *The Nearly Man*.

# 6.

# A TOUCH OF CLASS

MIDDLESEX won the county championship again almost immediately Murray retired. After 27 barren years, it was a moment of such triumph that even the normally fastidious Mike Brearley was seen clad only in a towel and chugging champagne from the bottle following the team's climactic win against Surrey at the Oval. He was surrounded by a talented pool of players like the now 43-year-old Fred Titmus, Clive Radley, Graham Barlow, Phil Edmonds and Mike Selvey, while the reserves contained Mike Gatting, John Emburey and others who would become first-team regulars. The county fielded no fewer than four alternating wicketkeepers during the season, the teenaged Ian Gould eventually emerging from the pack. It was the beginning of a golden era in Middlesex's fortunes in which they won five pennant races and four one-day trophies in ten seasons, and Brearley once said of it:

> 'The group I took over in 1971 wasn't conducive to good team spirit. I tried to change that, and some of the older players didn't much like it.'

He added:

> 'John Murray was a terrific man and a wonderful keeper, but he'd clearly learnt his cricket at a different time, when the captain was a god and you didn't dare express an opinion until you'd put in ten years as a capped player.'

In the new, egalitarian Middlesex dressing-room, Phil Edmonds would soon revel in the name 'Margaret' – leader of the opposition – and in time even the veteran Titmus remarked approvingly that 'there was a lot more genuine debate, and a better atmosphere as a whole, than when Murray, Parfitt and I ran things. A lightbulb went off for some of us in the mid-1970s: What we did to be good before wasn't good enough anymore.'

Murray was typically self-effacing when I put all this to him. 'Well,' he said after a suitable pause, 'at least now Middlesex knew what they'd been doing wrong for the last 25 years. They'd obviously never make a go of it with me in the side.'

After toying with the idea of becoming an umpire, or a full-time coach, Murray let such matters drop, and turned to a life of gardening, golfing, raising his family and continuing to travel as a rep for Derrick Robins's Banbury Squash Courts firm. He was awarded the MBE in the 1976 New Year's Honours list, and was unimpressed when a certain titled individual associated with Banbury wrote to congratulate him: 'I understand that you have been with us for a while as a junior representative, and I hope I will have an opportunity of meeting you at some time.' Murray thought this 'bloody typical' of the proconsular management attitude prevalent in 1970s British industrial relations, which made the atmosphere of the average county cricket dressing-room seem positively folksy by comparison. There was some further talk about a book, too, and a tabloid newspaper enquired about his putting his name to an occasional column. It all came to nothing: Murray wasn't the sort of retired cricketer to metaphorically spit his teeth into his hand and come out swinging about what was wrong with the modern game – and, besides, 'It's bloody hard graft, this writing,' he once told me.

It's easy to get depressed thinking of Murray suddenly having to scratch a living as a sales rep, although he assured me that he hadn't missed the sheer grind of seven-days-a-week cricket in the least, and, anyway, he still looked in at Lord's whenever he could. Fred Titmus told me in this context that 'JT walked in to the Long Room bar with me once in 1976 or '77, and some of the old boys fairly sputtered into their gins and acted like they were schoolkids again when they saw him.' It was ever thus for Murray (whom Middlesex invited to make a one-match comeback at the end of the 1976 season and thus qualify for a championship winners' medal, an offer he politely declined), who went on to work for Slazenger and to serve for several years as treasurer of the Cricketers' Association. Around 1980 he joined Godfrey Evans, Ted Dexter and Fred Trueman on the panel of the Gordon's Gin Wicketkeeper of the Month award, which if nothing else proved agreeable for its extended lunchtime selection meetings. After one of these Murray strolled up Baker Street in the late-afternoon sunshine, passed through the Grace Gates and in to the Lord's pavilion, where he knocked on the door of the Middlesex dressing-room. One of the junior players opened it, and invited the old keeper in. Fred Titmus wasn't playing in that particular match, and as a result the place was strangely quiet. Murray looked around for a moment at the largely unfamiliar faces staring back at him. The sponsor's product had flowed pretty freely at lunch that day. 'I just want to say one thing,' he remarked at length, in his dry, throaty voice. 'I don't think you've peaked yet. Your best days are ahead of you. I know you can do even bigger and better things.'

It was the sort of plain, unassuming address Murray did best. He always scrupulously avoided anything 'clever' in his public remarks, and never much cared for the after-dinner circuit that provides certain former players with the opportunity of self-advertisement. There was a moment's silence. Then the room, whether as a show of affirmation, or in a tribute to the speaker of these words, erupted in cheers.

Not long after his retirement from Middlesex, Murray and his family moved out of London to a small house in the Surrey countryside – not exactly the far side of the moon, but another clear sign that his playing days were over. As he wrote to an old Test colleague that Christmas, '[Cricket] is like a page I've turned over', although he still flicked through the closing scores in his newspaper each morning, and still went up to Lord's whenever he had a spare hour to do so. Murray genuinely liked being around most cricket people. He just didn't have such a compelling need for their company, on a daily basis, that he actively sought a way of getting back in to the game.

Then, of all people, the England selectors came calling. By the spring of 1977 Murray's friend Alec Bedser had been in the chair for eight long seasons, generally unremarkable ones for the national game as a whole, at least until the leaked announcement early that May of the Australian media tycoon Kerry Packer's World Series Cricket. Overnight, it was bedlam. 'Cricket "Circus" Threat to Test Matches' ran the comparatively subdued headline in *The Times*, while extra-bold, war-is-declared type and multiple exclamation marks typified the coverage elsewhere. Those first reports suggested that Packer was planning a tournament between Australia and the rest, that England's captain Tony Greig and his team-mates Derek Underwood, Alan Knott and John Snow had all signed up, and that the matches would be played in 'unconventional format'. That was putting it mildly: Packer eventually hired 70 players from around the world for 16 'Supertests' and 38 day-night games staged over two seasons, which among other things featured coloured kit, helmets, yellow (later white) balls, floodlights and drop-in pitches grown in greenhouses. Although the active phase of the revolution ended in a compromise in 1979, nothing was ever quite the same again. At a time when the Test and County Cricket Board under the chairmanship of Doug Insole paid its senior players £180 for each five-day Test match, Packer forcefully reminded the game's officials that it was the stars, not them, who put fans in the seats. That's a point a Joe Root or a Ben Stokes still make today, every time they collect their million-pound annual retainer or their £15,000 basic Test match fee.

Meanwhile, a small sea-change had also come over Len Hutton, what he later called a kind of 'general gloom about life'. The former England captain had been a Test selector since May 1975, but remarked that it had been a 'stingy' and 'increasingly difficult' post to fulfil, particularly in light of what he characterised as the 'Packer claptrap' and Geoff Boycott's earlier decision to make himself unavailable for England. Hutton took exception to the approaches certain of his co-selectors made to persuade Boycott to change his mind. 'No one should have to be forced to play cricket for his country,' he once told me. Hutton also confirmed that he wasn't fond of the committee side of the job, and in that uniquely turbulent early summer of 1977 he finally stood down in favour of Murray.

The first full fruit of this new appointment, the 1977/78 England tour under Mike Brearley's captaincy of Pakistan and New Zealand, was a mixed success. As Alex Bannister put it in *Wisden*:

> 'If judged solely by a playing record of only one victory in six Tests, a first-ever defeat by New Zealand, and two drawn series, England's winter could be dismissed as a failure.'

Set against this, 22-year-old Ian Botham emerged as what Bannister called 'a considerable all-rounder with a pugnacious attitude', Bob Taylor kept wicket well in Knott's absence, and even Boycott at long last returned to the fold. Murray thought it all a 'pretty good start'. He didn't know that within less than a year he was to be wrenched from the shadowy obscurity of the cricket administrator, and once again find himself plastered over the back pages in connection to a Test-selection dispute.

Pakistan and New Zealand in turn toured England in the miserably wet summer of 1978. Botham got a lot of wickets and batsmen like Graham Gooch and David Gower were coming in to their own. Still 'all quite satisfactory', said Murray, who may have done his one really imperishable thing as a national selector late that summer, which was to have opened the England dressing-room door at Trent Bridge one afternoon to see a 'shaggy-haired bloke in a neon-green suit, with about half a dozen leggy birds standing chattering behind him, telling me that the captain had invited him in'. It was Mick Jagger. Murray told him that he was welcome to come in without his entourage, and at that the Rolling Stones vocalist had promptly dismissed them, going on to spend a couple of hours sitting decorously on the players' balcony. 'He was quite a different guy with his gang than he was with us – kept pouring people cups of tea and saying how much he wished he could have been a cricketer.' The women returned to the door in high spirits at the close of play, and Jagger went off to join them with a sheepish grin – 'rather a shy, suburban bloke under all the clobber ... He looked like a parrot that had just flown into a freshly-painted wall,' Murray later wrote to me, as acute a judgement of that particular subject as any rock author could wish for. Alec Bedser had happened to pass the distinguished visitor, then in his 15th year of global notoriety, in the doorway, but apparently had trouble placing him. 'Who the fuck was that?' he asked Murray. Murray told him. 'Never heard of him,' said Bedser.

Here's what Murray told me about the subsequent selection meeting to choose the 16 England players to tour Australia in 1978/79:

> 'We came down to the second wicketkeeper position after Bob Taylor. We talked about David Bairstow for a while, and then we talked about Paul Downton. They were by a mile the best two candidates. We're about to vote on it and suddenly Mike Brearley says, "I don't want a second keeper sitting around on his backside all winter – we need someone who can play as a batsman, and I'm nominating Roger Tolchard." Really? Well, by this stage I notice that George Mann and my friend Doug Insole from the TCCB are also sitting there – never seen either one of them in a selection meeting before – and Insole immediately calls for a vote, and it goes Brearley's way. So Tolchard went to Australia, where as I recall he played two or three matches during the whole tour. Very nice bloke, and a perfectly competent stopper – just not my choice to be representing England.'

Murray himself immediately resigned his position on a point of principle, having not for the first time fallen foul of the modern love affair with the wicketkeeper-batsman. 'I thought, if they don't want to listen to my opinion about keepers, I've really got no reason to be here. So that was the end of me as a selector.'

* * *

There's something uniquely gloomy about watching cricketers of a certain age come out of retirement to go through their paces one more time, even, as in the case of the Courage Old England XI of the 1980s, for as worthy a cause as the National Grocers' Benevolent Trust or the Licensed Victuallers' Association fund for handicapped children. It's a shock for the spectator. One moment, it seems, you're adoring your immaculately smooth idols as they swan about the park in their blazers and flannels, and the next they're slouching around with beer-guts and dodgy hairlines, pretending they still care, and your long-term lease in the realm of eternal youth has well and truly been given its eviction notice. Like rock music, professional sport's standard currency has always been aspirational fantasy, not nuanced reality. In this same connection, I occasionally used to watch Denis Compton playing village cricket in his mid-fifties, and it was somehow both a melancholy and a laugh-out-loud funny experience, often even intentionally so. While in the field, cricket's one-time glamour boy generally stood rather informally at slip, where he dropped an impressive number of catches, and when the moment came seemed to be only dimly familiar with the manufacturer's suggested uses for the mysterious lump of wood he now held in his hands. It was all a bit like visiting a once magnificent old palace whose roof had caved in.

So Murray chose his few post-retirement appearances carefully. He was well aware of the self-inflicted humiliations suffered by the middle-aged public performer, either paunchy and chinless, or stuffed liked a sausage into their girdle, as they lumber out among us. He was far too proud and self-aware for such indignities. He was also sustainable. For all Murray's wonderful style and poise, which seemed to place him out of time, he'd always managed to resist the cult of youth that Compton and others built and were then entrapped by. 'The great thing is that I was never really young,' Murray once told me, with a characteristic gravelly laugh. 'I mean, I was no oil painting. I was never going to be offered a job by Brylcreem, like Compo was,' he added, running a hand through his sparse hair. 'It's a big advantage in a way, because I think when I played those games in my forties I still looked and kept wicket pretty much like I did in my twenties. Obviously it's a more relaxed atmosphere, but I still never wanted to embarrass myself. I don't think I did.'

Nor do I. Turning out for the Duchess of Norfolk's team against the touring West Indies at Arundel in May 1980, the 45-year-old keeper was still good enough to stump Viv Richards when the opportunity presented itself, and later to smack a four back over Michael Holding's head. And, yes, they were both really trying. Two years later, at the Oval, Murray similarly dispatched both the World XI's openers, Bobby Simpson and Farokh Engineer, in quick order: 'Still his nimble self,' Swanton wrote, 'while others moved through the field looking as though their boot-laces were tied together.' It all ended at the same south London venue on 17 September 1983. Murray neither batted nor took a dismissal in the crushing Old England win over Garry Sobers's invitation side. Nor did he concede a bye. 'I was bloody tired at the end, though,' he admitted. 'I just went upstairs, changed, had a beer with Fred Trueman, and drove myself home again to the family. And that was it for me and the old gauntlets.'

Having made his debut more than 30 years earlier, when cricket was still known fondly as the 'gentleman's game', Murray had survived to see a time of lost certainties and frenetic, floodlit slogs between teams in fluorescent tracksuits. The arc of his career spanned more change in the sport than had been seen in any previous period of its history. My own favourite statistic remains the lower-order batsman's career Test record against the West Indies: one match, one innings, 112 runs, average 112. Since Murray once genially remarked that 'Charlie Elliott giving me out lbw that day [in 1966] was the worst decision I ever got in 25 years as a professional cricketer' (he'd still walked immediately), he could just as easily have ended up with the distinctly useful median of infinity against what was then arguably the world's strongest bowling attack. Even so, 112 is more than double the figure that any one of Colin Cowdrey, Tom Graveney, Ken Barrington, Ted Dexter or Compton himself managed during their years of facing the West Indies. They may have appeared in more matches than Murray did, but it's still a gloriously indelible footnote to the career of a wicketkeeper who supposedly 'couldn't bat' at that level.

Even the relentless Geoff Boycott achieved a lifetime average of only 45 against that particular opposition. Jim Parks and Alan Knott managed 26 and 29 respectively.

* * *

To many people, entering the mid-level corporate workforce after a quarter of a century of playing professional sport around the world might have appeared depressing. But Murray never seemed to mind it. Possibly there was even something about it that appealed to the efficiency expert in him.

While England's former wicketkeeper drove around the country first selling squash courts and then Slazenger sports products, I left Cambridge, got married and divorced, and ended up working, if it could be called that, in the bowels of a London public relations agency. This was the eighties, and some of my colleagues there liked to refer to themselves as being in 'the media', a boast not untainted by an implied, though unjustified, claim to some sort of creative status. PR as I experienced it back then related to the media, let alone the arts, in the sense that the jockstrap washer relates to a first-class cricket team, although along the way I at least managed to get a toehold in the sports writing world – yearbooks and brochures, the occasional 'colour piece' for the nationals – and by the spring of 1989 was polishing off a biography of my recurrent houseguest Godfrey Evans. One way or another, I thought of myself as hardened to the whole childish business of hero-worship. Working with Evans – again, I use the verb loosely – had widened my horizons. I got used to meeting Denis Compton or Keith Miller for lunch. My secretary once passed me a note saying, 'Ted Dexter phoned about England selection' (the team's, alas, not my own). Evans himself spent weekends on my sofa, which he once managed to set on fire. In short I was semi-gainfully employed in the game I loved, paid to meet famous cricketers over drinks and translate their thoughts on to paper.

This was exactly what I was doing on the warm evening of Tuesday, 23 May 1989, wedged between Evans and an impressively belligerent Tony Lock, the latter vowing to stop a certain 'MCC cunt' (he won't be named) from addressing the room, by whatever means it took, at Brian Statham's glittering benefit dinner at the Grosvenor House in London. As mentioned, they were all there that night. Apart from Evans and Lock, there were former greats of the game who defined cricket as physical (Frank 'Typhoon' Tyson), graceful (Tom Graveney) and intense (Len Hutton). Peter May, Alec Bedser and Trevor Bailey all sat less than a pitch-length away, and in time Fred Trueman got up to do a revue that turned 'arse' (no ladies were present that night) into the longest one-syllable drawl in comedic history, and then went on from there to get a bit lewd. Later in the proceedings the elderly Gubby Allen shuffled by leaning on the arm of E.W. Swanton and told me he'd quite enjoyed a short profile of Evans I'd sent in, unsolicited, to the *Cricketer*, and instead of accepting it as the random drunken remark at a party it was I remember treating it as a sort of papal blessing. Godders himself wanted to get out and lose some more money at the nearby Sportsman Club's casino before it closed, and since I was again putting him up for the night I went with him. The old Kent stumper was turning 70 about then, and in fine spirits, looking fine, too, square and solid with Picwickian whiskers. His suntan from a recent paid Easter break in Barbados gave him a wizened, Native American sort of look in a professionally styled photograph taken that night of the nine surviving members of the England side that won back the Ashes at the Oval in 1953. Despite the whiskers, up close the great stumper looked every inch the boisterous inner teenager he really was, and I knew that we were still in for a long night at the casino, again failing to win the millions that were eternally promised but somehow never materialised as a result of Godders's patented 'system' at the roulette table, and then sitting up late over the cooking brandy at my little place in Hammersmith.

As we were pushing our way through the sea of cummerbunds towards the exit, I happened to look over at a table set up in the far corner of the ballroom, a kitchen door banging in to its outermost chair, and counted off the still-familiar faces sitting there: Russell, Parfitt, Edrich, Titmus and ... The next thing I remember is asking Evans, in a voice a full octave higher than usual, to introduce us. John Murray actually stood up to shake my hand.

We lingered there for a minute or two, exchanging pleasantries, Evans, having pocketed the menu his England successor had just autographed for him, giving me the international sign for 'Snap it up' from over Murray's shoulder, but I must have at least extracted a phone number because I recall waiting the statutory minimum time for a first date and then ringing to ask JT, as I now called him, out to lunch. 'When's good for you?' he immediately replied. Even during that brief encounter at the Grosvenor, it rapidly bore in on me that Murray wasn't quite the same proposition up close he'd been on public view. He was better. At the end of our first short interview I was struck by my hero's unfeigned smile, the teeth prominent and widely spaced, but bared in all the cheery innocence of a 1960s ring-of-confidence Colgate commercial. He was suddenly, wonderfully, a young man. I felt about 11 again.

The character I got to know at the surprisingly unpretentious little lunch place in Holborn with communal benches and a beer garden out back was extraordinarily kind and modest, and endured with exceptional grace the inevitable moments when some fellow middle-aged fan would appear unbidden at our table and announce himself by saying, 'You won't remember me, John, but I was in the Ansell stand at Edgbaston when ...' One evening in the summer of 1989 or 1990 I arranged to properly interview Murray for a small article I was doing on England's post-war wicketkeepers. (Aside from his many other qualities, I soon discovered that my idol had marvellous recall, and could talk easily and affectionately about otherwise forgotten players whom he'd known on the way up, 40 years earlier.) We agreed to meet at the Cricketers Club in Baker Street at six that evening, and at seven we were being joined by an American friend of mine who was in London to research a book of some sort she was writing about Arthur Conan Doyle, whom (the woman, not Doyle) I was then taking on to dinner. Though highly estimable in her way, I should mention that this individual knew nothing about cricket. In so far as the name John Murray meant anything to her it was as the imprint of the firm that had published *The Case-Book of Sherlock Holmes,* whose fictional home lay just up the road from where we sat. Anyway, she arrived a few minutes early and joined us at our table. After introducing everyone, I went to the bar for another round of drinks. I remember the author wanted something involving frozen Polish vodka and a sugar cube, with what looked like a mini-Japanese flag impaled on a lemon slice in it, and John requested a glass of house red. After that we sat there for a while talking about books. It was only a day or two later that I realised I'd left my tape-recorder running on the table while I was at the bar and when I played this back I could hear my American friend expounding on her new project for a while, followed by her casually asking Murray: 'Did you ever play cricket yourself?' 'Oh, on and off,' he said, in a level voice.

For one reason or another I spent a fair amount of my time loitering at that same club during the early 1990s. After I wrote my book on Godfrey Evans I did one on Tom Graveney, and after that there was some loose talk about a Compton biography that in the end didn't happen (I solaced the void by turning to Murray's friend Mick Jagger), but still involved some enjoyably protracted getting-acquainted sessions with the man himself at the Baker Street venue, situated conveniently close to the advertising agency where, Denis informed us, he 'sometimes looked in' for an hour or so on weekday afternoons. In my case, the usual routine was that I'd present myself at the club at around noon, and then reel back home again sometime between the tea interval and the close of play. Compton would operate as a sort of one-man cottage industry while on the premises, surrounded by a seemingly endless stream of admirers, the attention he gave to friend and fan alike tempered only by his concern for the result of the 3.45 at Uttoxeter showing on the television above the bar. Looking back on the era I'm rightly conscious of mixed emotions at the way I conducted my life as a whole, but I can at least say that I struck one unequivocal blow for good during my early thirties, and that this involved arranging for Compton, Evans, Graveney and Murray to sit down together one day for lunch.

Although I hesitate to distil each of these four superbly accomplished and in their own ways not uncomplicated individuals on the basis of one well-oiled meal together, it's fair to say that Compton was the most naturally gregarious of the group, and probably also the one most aware of his own reputation, telling us of a black-tie affair he'd just attended where 'the PM kept bringing me drinks like he was the ruddy waiter'. Compo's face, by then richly tinted at the best of times, flushed with joy at the thought of it. Evans was typically loud, indiscreet and fun, although the sheer amount of gin he put away sometimes worried people until they got to know him, at which point it worried them even more. Graveney was an extremely affable soul whose family was unfailingly kind to me at the time I wrote my book about him. Of course he'd had his own ups and downs in cricket, and I remember he once told me after I'd read out a purple passage someone wrote extolling the matchless beauty of his batting that I should balance this eulogy by seeking the views of 'one of the many people around who dislike me'. More than most, perhaps, he focused on the negative, and in so doing he could, in his darker moments, perceive anything short of a rave as a put-down.

Murray was simply the most natural and unaffected of the four great cricketers at the table. I noticed how he only rarely allowed himself to intrude on anyone else's story, even when he himself happened to be featured in it. While Evans explained how the top-class wicketkeeper should link his little fingers together when taking the ball, Compton reminisced about the Middlesex dressing-room of the 1950s, and Graveney recalled the vagaries of Doug Insole and his co-selectors, Murray just sat there smiling benignly. It was as though it had nothing particularly to do with him, merely that he was taking it all in. You marvelled again at his innate modesty and his disinclination ever to speak ill of anyone.

That's not to say he was a pushover. He once told me that he always thought there were too many 'twats' at Lord's interfering with matters better left to players, and that this regrettable state of affairs never really changed. He may have been the most genial of all professional cricketers, but there was no way he was going to let the buggers tell him what to do.

Murray had his own coping technique for sidestepping pointed or inconvenient questions. If you asked him about something controversial like the England selection panel, he'd laugh and then soliloquise at length on a series of topics, starting off with one not altogether unrelated to the subject at hand, before shading off into others of diminishing relevance, until finally he was on safe ground, telling you again about how truly lucky he felt ever to have been picked by England in the first place, and that Jim Parks and Alan Knott (I gave him every conversational prompt I possibly could over the course of 30 years to denounce one or both of these rivals for the selectors' affections) were in fact wonderful keepers and extremely nice chaps to boot.

An old lady who had cooked the players' lunches at Lord's during much of the 1960s once told me that Murray had gone out of his way to thank her for her work at the time, and to ask her about how some of her best dishes – usually involving roast beef or some other English staple – were prepared. Though she suspected that charm was at work – even flattery – she was also struck by the obvious care with which Murray listened to her. 'It may have been half out of politeness, but I always got the feeling he was storing it all up for future use,' a theory confirmed by those of us lucky enough to have sat at the Murrays' dinner table in later years. With her, as with so many others, he knew what he was doing.

I never kept score, but Murray and I probably met three or four times a year between 1989 and 1996. I would have liked it to be more often, but I was also wary of coming over the hot-cheeked schoolboy with him again, forgetting myself and doing something rash like inviting him to be godfather to my first child. During those years Murray still went to Lord's whenever he could – he remained a Middlesex man to his core – and I remember he once rang me largely to enthuse about a young player he'd just seen score 80 or so for the county seconds, who turned out to be Andrew Strauss. He also continued to represent Slazenger, and once persuaded the firm to put some lucrative work Geoff Boycott's way – 'typically generous of John, who always looked after his mates', the Yorkshireman told me. Later Murray and his cousin went in together as partners in the security-guard trade (with the slogan 'We Mind Your Business'), although he told me good-naturedly that this had involved him 'sitting around the office doing the accounts, or taking clients out to lunch, [rather than] wading in to sort out some character in a balaclava turning over the local bank'.

One morning in the early summer of 1995, Murray told me on the phone that he'd had the lurgy, or flu, but would be going up to Lord's to watch the Friday of the Test with the West Indies. I met him there. As we were walking round the back of the Warner Stand towards the pavilion, close to the spot where I'd once gazed up slack-jawed at John as he passed by me in his England blazer, we saw an animated little procession coming our way. When we were a few yards apart I noticed that it included both the Queen and our old mutual friend Dennis Silk, who, with a certain inevitability, was by then serving as Insole's successor as chairman of the Test and County Cricket Board. As I looked from one luminary to the other, and then back again, I wasn't immediately sure whether to modestly avert my gaze, smile, or bow – and, if the last, to whom? A kind of scarcely perceptible scowl had crossed my old headmaster's face as he saw us, although he gave no other sign of recognising in Murray one of the men he'd led on tour of New Zealand 35 years earlier. Perhaps protocol didn't permit it. Either way, he and his party passed through the pavilion door and out of our sight. Murray gave it a moment, and then looked at me. 'Who was that woman with Mr Silk?' he asked. After that a boy of about ten walked up to us with a pen and an autograph book. Then there were half a dozen others, some brandishing scorecards, others with bulky mobile phones, in a tight little scrum around the pavilion doorstep. Murray may not have suddenly gathered thousands of impressionable youths around him on *Catcher in the Rye* level, but he certainly had a small collection of young fans.

No one said anything. The boys just thrust the proffered material at Murray. He was extremely gracious about it all, signing and posing for several minutes. 'Their dads must have put them up to it,' he smiled, as the gang dispersed, and I did the mental arithmetic. Murray had then just turned 60, and had already been retired for 20 years. It would have been like me in 1967, the season of *Their Satanic Majesties* and sundry pop-star drug busts, thrilling to the latest jukebox hits by Ethel Merman or Johnny Mercer in his 'Zip-a-Dee-Doo-Dah' phase. We went in to the Long Room to watch the match. Angus Fraser was bowling to Carl Hooper, Alec Stewart behind the stumps. After a while I asked Murray what he thought of England's latest batting wicketkeeper. 'Nice, steady lad,' he said affably. 'No frills. All he cares about is stopping the ball.'

And that's all he did.

Later that year, I moved (temporarily, so I thought) to Seattle, and when I mentioned this fact to Murray he sent me an over-generous letter saying he would miss our lunches together, but hoping that I would 'Be lucky – and be sure to drop us a line to let us know what you're up to,' before adding that he would think of me whenever he looked in at the Cricketers Club. I don't suppose he did, but I warmed to the convivial thought. We had time for one more meal together before I got on the plane. At the end of it I handed Murray a picture of him, flanked by Garry Sobers and several others, leaving the field in triumph after his 1966 century against the West Indies, with the request that he autograph it. He wrote: 'Dear Chris, My grandchildren are very impressed that I know the biographer of Mick Jagger, Clapton + Bowie – not at all impressed that the lot on my left are mates!! Cheers, John.'

* * *

That wasn't quite the end, though. I got in the habit of coming back each spring, and right after I did so I'd ring Murray and suggest we meet. After about the third year in a row this had happened, he said one day on the phone, 'Why not come down to dinner at the house?', and gave me directions. It was the beginning of what I like to think of as the best phase of the friendship. Around six o'clock I'd get off the packed commuter train, experiencing some of the old schoolboy knee-wobble as I did so, at the Murrays' station. There, unbelievably, would be JT, precisely dressed, as always, waiting to shake my hand. But then that hand wasn't released. Still holding it, Murray would grin, and, whatever your mood had been up until then, you grinned back. He would tell you how unchanged you looked, and enquire after your family members by name. After that he'd go on to ask whether you happened to have seen the latest Middlesex score, and as he drove off at some speed down the narrow English lanes the next topic under discussion would be something like: 'What do you think about Geraint Jones, then?' This seemed like a perfectly logical subject to raise with Murray, who, after all, knew a thing or two about young Kent wicketkeepers breaking in to the England Test side. But it was John himself who was asking the question. And then you'd be off, merrily lecturing the greatest specialist player of his generation on the supposed defects of his England successors, while John himself just quietly sat there, apparently rapt with attention at your profound insights on the subject. It was like telling Tolstoy about the short story on the amusing social changes arising out of some local war you were thinking of submitting to the weekly freesheet. John's face never registered anything but good-natured interest on these occasions.

The house itself was, of course, immaculately neat, very English, with a view over a rolling green communal lawn and a small wood colonised by foxes. There was little evidence that anyone living there had ever been a famous cricketer, although from time to time, when a name like Bailey or Bedser or Hutton cropped up, John would excuse himself and come back in again a minute later with the relevant edition of *Wisden* in his hand. He and the wonderfully patient Colleen celebrated their golden anniversary in 2008. They were both kind, cheerful and interested, and loved to make jokes and reminisce. No one that I ever knew was nicer to me.

I still tried to impress him. Each year I brought down a new book I'd written during the winter and handed it over with what I hoped passed for a suitably bashful grin. Murray sometimes asked me to sign them. It cheered me up to do so the way collecting John's autograph had cheered me up years before. What I chiefly remember is the way he had of holding his head slightly to one side with an encouraging smile on his face as you launched in to your latest well-worn 1960s cricket story, and the sheer joy, possibly not untinged by relief, of his laughter when you finished it. He never had a truly unkind word to say about any of his former colleagues or opponents, never seemed to forget himself, and always spoke calmly and precisely, as though every sentence had to pay its way. My own guess is that he liked stability and order in his life, and was prepared to do what it took to keep them.

'What was Sobers like, John, in his prime?' 'Sobers?' he'd say. 'Not too shabby. Lovely swing bowler, not so hot with the spin. He could murder you batting. I remember MCC against the West Indies at Lord's in '66, and old Peter Walker bowling slow left-arm from the top end. Well, he let Sobers have two or three balls, and it looked like Garry was in real trouble with them, shuffling around like he'd never held a bat in his hands before. And after each one he'd call up the wicket, "Well bowled, Pete." So Walker gave him the exact same treatment again, and this time Garry banged it into the middle deck of the pavilion. No change of expression. "Well bowled, Pete." Lovely bloke, too, always smiling whatever was going on in the middle.' Murray failed to mention that he'd scored an unbeaten century in that same match, but I once had the good luck to ask Sobers about it. 'John was the best English keeper I ever played against,' he said simply. 'And if they say he couldn't bat I'd like to know what they think he was doing that day at Lord's against Charlie Griffith, Wes Hall and me.'

'What about Lock and Laker?' I once asked Murray, jumping around in the order a bit, possibly because at the time I was trying to find someone to publish a dual biography of the Surrey spin twins. 'Lovely bowler, Jim,' he said after a slight pause. 'Bit of an enigma. We had a whip-round for him once at Lord's, before a county game. It was Laker's benefit year, you see. Well, the Surrey boys turned up at the ground that morning, but no Jim. They said he'd hurt his finger somehow. Very bitter about it, they were. You heard a few harsh words uttered in his direction now and then. Lovely bowler, though.

'Lock?' Murray continued. 'I liked Lock. Not everyone did. Had a habit of walking around starkers in the dressing-room a bit too freely for some people's taste. Then there was always some new family waiting for him at the close of play, I remember. Wonderful bowler, though, great trier – he'd go at it all day if he had to.' Around 1993 dozens of former cricketers all over England each received a letter appealing for funds to support Lock in his criminal trial for allegedly molesting a teenaged Australian girl. While many of these same players were suddenly remembering that they had unexpected expenses that month and thus sadly couldn't help, Murray promptly sent a cheque. 'You always needed to encourage Laker to bowl,' he once told me. 'It was the opposite with Tony. The problem was getting the ruddy ball away from him.'

'Who were the best captains you played under?' I asked. 'Brian Close was brilliant on the field. Churchillian. Never surrender, that sort of thing,' Murray said. 'Bit of a handful in civvy street, I understand. Cowdrey and Mike Smith were both very nice blokes, not sure if you'd absolutely trust them with your life in a crisis. John Warr did a good job at Middlesex in the late '50s. People always talk about him as this sort of wisecracking toff, very droll with the after-dinner speeches and all that, but I tell you he could dish out the bollockings if he had to, one or two of them quite rich stuff, I recall. A good all-round skipper, John, on every level.

'Of course,' Murray added, 'I liked old Bill Edrich a lot. Gave me my county cap. But he put it away a bit, Bill, my word he did. He went out there at Lord's once to toss up at the start of play and he was leaning on the other lot's captain just to get out to the middle and back. Staggered in again, said "We're batting", went out about 20 minutes later, first man down, and scored a ton.' Murray agreed that his Middlesex colleague's core approach to life owed something to his experience as a wartime RAF bomber pilot. Edrich's courtship technique, in particular, impressively brisk at the best of times, had acquired a new urgency once death had stalked the scene. 'Still,' Murray said, 'it's not like he was exactly a monk before the war. Compton always swore they once found Bill sleeping it off with a blonde round the back of the groundsman's hut a few minutes before play began one day in

'38 or '39. He still had his dinner jacket on, or at least they were using it as a blanket, although he'd managed to lose his false teeth. Went out and scored a ton then, too.'

Murray said all this in his customary dry, slightly raspy voice, which I might add frequently dissolved in to fits of laughter. He was never spiteful in his judgements. Socially conservative (we never talked politics), he clearly wasn't one of those who think that freedom to tittle-tattle about other people's sex lives or to traffic in their private misery are keystones of the liberties which John Milton, John Wilkes and John Stuart Mill won for us. In many ways he was simply, and agreeably, old-fashioned. I'm ashamed to say that after a third or fourth glass of wine one night I started to enlighten Murray about the modern world's pathological aversion to boredom – most people I know can't even cross the street without their iPhone for company – and that this fact explained why so few customers were willing to endure the delayed gratification of a four- or five-day cricket match. 'You may be right,' he said in his usual friendly tone. 'But the long form is still best, and I don't think you'll find too many empty seats at any of the big Tests.' I felt like a fool. About an hour later, John was driving me back in the pitch dark to the house where I was staying. 'I know what you mean about one-day cricket,' he said quietly, out of nowhere. A few minutes later, we turned a corner and suddenly looked up to see the vast pink-neon sign and illuminated, G-stringed mannequins of the Ann Summers sex-shop world headquarters staring back at us. A bit incongruous here in rural Surrey, I remarked. 'Oh, we're very go-ahead in these parts,' said John, with a dry laugh at the thought. I think that was the night when I began to see him as the best living role-model of how to be a sane adult in the modern world. It wasn't anything to do with politics, just a peculiar frame of mind that was nostalgic for a vanished England. He simply absorbed it all, quietly amused by the coarseness of life, unswervingly true to his own values. I know for a fact that he fulfilled the most fundamental duty of a host, always showing respect to those under his roof, making them feel comfortable and cared for.

Sometimes it felt like I was performing a bit, or at least it did to me. Narcissistically, I got in the habit of replaying each of our meetings in my head, repeating the lines Murray would have heard, seeing the whole thing from his point of view. One year I was writing an article about John, so I made a note of our conversation and what I read through later came as a shock. In fact, it was often hard not to cringe – it was largely me talking about matches in which Murray had played and I'd read about or, at best, dimly recalled watching on TV. It may be a natural thing to do when you meet one of your idols, but it's about as sensible a tactic in terms of getting a genuine conversation going as facing Wes Hall or Charlie Griffith at their fastest without a box. As I say, Murray was always extremely cordial, laughing uproariously at stories he must have heard dozens of times before. Everything always seemed to go smoothly each time we met. When, dropping me off at the station, he looked steadily at me and said, 'It's good to see you again, mate,' I should have just taken him at his word instead of constantly worrying that I was making a fool of myself by behaving like a 60-year-old groupie who was overdoing it with all the second-hand cricket yarns. That's how I should have handled it – acceptance – if I'd been functioning as a fully rational adult, although if I'd been functioning that way I probably would never have had the pleasure of meeting Murray in the first place.

Looking back, I might just tentatively hazard that under Murray's supremely affable public persona and all the practised chattiness with strangers there was a more private and essentially unknowable side to him that owed something to his having grown up in the circumstances he did in the Britain of the 1940s. Several of his old colleagues remarked on this trait. Fred Titmus, who knew Murray better than most, affectionately remembered that there was 'a sort of screen' his friend had kept up, and that probably only his closest family members had ever penetrated it. Murray always seemed to take both good and bad turns of events in the same calmly undemonstrative manner. When in July 1962 Colin Cowdrey passed on the news that he was being recalled to the England team after a lengthy period in the international wilderness, the wicketkeeper's entire response was an uninflected, perfectly indifferent 'Oh'. Even when the terrible day came five years later and a *Daily Express* reporter rang Murray at home one Sunday morning to tell him that he had again been dropped by the selectors and Alan Knott called up in his place, the outgoing England keeper (who had immediately known that it effectively spelt the end) had merely thanked his caller for the news and then politely expressed the hope that they would meet up for a drink sometime soon.

Several of Murray's own notes to me over the years showed that his charm and knack for concealment were both intact. Reading them through now I see that they much more often talked about me than they did about him. I'd long ago worshipped him as a superbly polished and imperturbable cricketer. Now it gradually dawned on me that these same qualities were just as apparent in Murray personally. Towards the end of his life, Cowdrey told me that he sometimes felt a pang of guilt that 'John was quite harshly treated' by the national selectors, but that through it all the wicketkeeper himself had been 'amazingly patient'. The cricket addict Harold Pinter captured the same quality in an apparently spontaneous phrase. He told me on the phone in 1999 that he admired both Murray's 'exuberant front' and 'heavily shrouded interior'. The future Nobel Prize winner and I had quickly agreed that one way or another JT was one of the greatest men of our time. He'd shown us how to play cricket, now he showed us how to live.

* * *

Once I went up to meet John and Colleen Murray slightly off our normal beat in Vancouver, British Columbia. They were travelling through Canada by train and I got a card saying, 'We'll be about 100 miles from you, sorry we can't make it any closer.' John's admirer the late Graham Hill might not have been disappointed by the speed with which I covered those hundred miles. At the border a friendly middle-aged immigration official wearing a turban asked me the purpose of my visit, and I said, truthfully enough, that I was there to have lunch with my all-consuming childhood idol. '*The* JT Murray?' he asked, when I told him the name. John roared with laughter when I mentioned it to him. On the whole I think he was pleased to be reminded of his far-flung fame from time to time, although by the same token he never took himself too seriously. I remember the three of us turning a corner in Vancouver and suddenly coming face to face with a leprous, red-brick building that looked as though it had taken a direct hit from a bomb, with weeds sprouting up through its cracked front doorstep, where a couple of sparingly-clad young women lay smoking, and above its grimy or broken ground-floor windows a half-lit mauve neon sign which read: 'Murray Hotel'.

'Nice to know they've immortalised one,' John said.

I know that when I used to get on that hot early-evening train at Victoria I was usually brooding on some recent variant of the fact that human existence is largely ugliness, disorder, suffering, quarrels and guilt. By the time I got to East Croydon the will to live had generally returned, and somewhere around Riddlesdown the clammy-handed prep school boy was back, and engaged in a struggle for predominance with his soured, middle-aged alter ego. Sometimes it all seemed faintly unreal, more like a dream, just to walk over the rickety tin bridge crossing the platforms at Murray's station and look down to see him standing there at attention next to the car, whatever the weather, waiting to greet me. Was it really the same unapproachable figure I'd worshipped from afar half a century earlier? Once I went down for dinner, the Murrays and I sat up talking, and eventually they enquired kindly if I might care to spend the night, and then, unbelievably, the next thing I heard was my own voice saying thanks very much, but I have to be in London first thing to see a publisher, and I should probably get back. I would have gnawed off a limb for that same invitation around the years 1966 and 1967. I still regret the folly of my decision, particularly since the publisher characteristically bailed on me.

Murray himself would have disowned any attempt to claim him as the greatest cricketer who ever lived, let alone as a philosopher of the sport, an innovator or a sage. 'You can say that if you like,' he once informed me, with a characteristic snort of laughter, when I grew over-effusive on the subject. 'But as far as I'm concerned I was just a bloke who got very, very lucky to be paid for doing what he loved.' He often told me that, in retirement, he was living the dream – plenty of golf, music, summer afternoons at Lord's (he spoke a lot about the parking arrangements, or lack of them) and of course his all-important family. Although he'd faded from public view, I sometimes watched him interact with one or two of those outside his inner circle. Once, sitting waiting in his car, Murray was seriously concerned because another motorist had suddenly walked up to him and taken his photograph. I tried to laugh it off by telling him the man was probably just another middle-aged fan, but John was worried that it all portended something bad. In some ways it seemed odd that the incident would have troubled him quite as much as it did, but he was always anxious to avoid the least hint of any possible strife or confrontation.

Another time we were sitting together in his house, the doorbell rang, and a small, beetle-browed man in a brown suit stood there announcing that he was a detective. Murray gave me a look. The man badged us, glanced professionally around the room, and sat down. The atmosphere changed perceptibly as he did so. You were suddenly aware of the proximity of the Establishment, the world of registered brown envelopes and dry official lips. The caller told us that he was investigating an attempted burglary nearby. Murray answered a few routine questions, all very formal, and made a nervous joke about unpaid parking tickets that could have gone better. Finally the rozzer flipped his notebook shut, looked long and hard at John, cleared his throat, and said, 'I've always wanted to ask you this, sir. When you were batting in that Test against the West Indies at the Oval ...' Next to me I could hear John exhale again. As we listened, the man went on and on about what a great game that had been – Murray and Graveney were so brilliant, each one effortlessly matching the other, the sun shining, England on top, and the small boy sitting with his sandwiches in the seats under the gasometer had 'never wanted it to end', he now told us.

In April 2015 one of my books was somehow shortlisted for an award and I asked Murray if he would be my guest for the event in the Lord's Long Room. He immediately agreed, although worried that he would be out of place among all the 'arty types' he might meet there. I kept telling him beforehand, accurately enough, that I wouldn't win, and about the third time I did so John looked at me reprovingly and said: 'You don't know that.' It was a well-earned rebuke. Looking back on it, I suppose it was the difference between the spurious, I'm-not-worthy reflex and the professional sportsman's spirit of eternal enterprise. Anyway, I didn't win. Murray, something of an expert on the ways of cricket dinners, cast a seasoned eye on the food when it came to our table. 'Ah, yes, that'll be the twenty quid menu – meat and two veg with pud, very nice, better than we had for the golf night – perhaps there's something in this book lark after all.' He signed a lot of autographs, told everyone of course he remembered them, feigned convincing interest in their cricket or golf stories, and asked politely if they were still playing. When the results came, John slapped me on the back, muttered

'Hard luck, mate' and poured me another glass of wine. I dimly sensed that there was a lesson to be learnt there somewhere. When Murray succeeded, he was gracious. When he failed, he remained quiet and even-tempered. A couple of weeks later, we were walking up a steep flight of steps outside his house and John paused for a moment, catching his breath. It was the first time I'd seen him even briefly out of sorts. We stood there, and then after a bit he looked at me and said quietly, 'That was a bloody good book you wrote.' I seriously doubt whether any other review could give me more pleasure.

In May 2018 I went back to my old school, St Aubyns. It had been closed down several years earlier, apparently destined for redevelopment as a seafront luxury assisted-living 'scheme', but you could still see the original granite pile looming up behind the builder's scaffolding. Never perhaps conventionally beautiful, it was now a study in threadbare melancholy. A doom seemed to have fallen on the central block, with its drooping roof and dank, peeling exterior walls, while the games field where my father had once stood in full dress uniform and I'd in turn lumbered around pretending to be John Murray now looked like a long-abandoned archaeological dig, covered in tall, luxuriant weeds and muddy bogs that seemed to offer the prospect of an outbreak of Lime Disease in the summer. The place wasn't exactly a pleasure-dome at the best of times, but walking around it in its semi-ruined state, while the rain dripped down, was a uniquely depressing experience. Later that evening I went to see Murray again. Everything was the same, except that he gave me an even longer handshake than usual as we parted at the station. 'Be lucky,' John said, with a wink. I watched him drive off in the dark.

A funny little thought kept running through my head. Had I said goodbye to both my remaining childhood icons on the same day?

I went back to Seattle and wrote a short story for some of the British papers about the Atlantic special relationship and more particularly Donald Trump's riotous first visit to London. The few friends who noticed it were polite, while apparently agreeing that my professed low opinion of it wasn't mock humility. In time Murray sent me an email which said: 'Have read your words of wisdom in the Sunday press. Great stuff. Never knew all that detail about the 1960s, and I was there! Very proud to be your latest subject. Cheers, JT.' He added that he was looking forward to seeing Middlesex play Warwickshire at Lord's a week or so later. 'Sun-kissed here, so the ball should be turning – fingers crossed for a home win!' he wrote. It was all characteristically generous and upbeat. John always worked hard at making connections with people, right up to the end, charming my son on the phone one day with a series of questions about major-league baseball which suggested he'd actually studied the subject in advance rather than just trotting out a few generic phrases about it. Murray cheerfully told me around then that he still had big plans, loved to travel, and wanted to see more of life. Perhaps he was racing, as we all are, against time. He might well have mocked the idea, but I always tried to see him in his full context, in the round, not just as another ex-cricketer, but more like an actor playing out his role, determined to amuse and inspire to the last, in that sense a man touched by the heroic. Sometimes it seemed like a dream that this once unattainable figure was still with us, living in suburban Surrey, and that I could idly turn on a computer or pick up a phone and be instantly connected to the man whose personal style and authority had more than anything else made my childhood worth living.

That particular dream ended with a message late on the night of Tuesday, 24 July 2018. Murray had gone to watch Middlesex play Warwickshire at Lord's, just as he'd said, having stopped en route to collect his significant winnings after backing the long shot Francesco Molinari to win the British Open. It was a great day all round. The sun shone and the home team won in a tight finish. John was back where it had all begun – the place where he'd brought off a total of 670 dismissals in his first-class career, among them a record six catches in a Test innings, as well as numerous other appearances on the lists for most victims in three-day and limited-over matches, and, more importantly, where it had started for him 68 years earlier when, as an eternally optimistic and ambitious apprentice cricketer, he'd walked through the top gate one spring morning to be promptly handed a broom and told to get on with it. One way or another, it seemed nearly his whole life had been spent in the shadow of the stately old ground: Murray had either been working there, or playing there, or in later years simply enjoying the spectacle there, and in between times 'Lord's' had sometimes come to be a synonym for cricket officialdom and more especially for the Test selectors whom many thought (though John himself never said so) had badly mistreated him. Now the circle had closed. As Murray was leaving his seat that warm late July evening he rang his family to say he had thoroughly enjoyed the day and would be back with them soon. He collapsed by the Harris Garden behind the pavilion. He was 83, had first fallen in love with cricket when he saw the touring Australians at Lord's almost exactly 70 years to the day earlier, and, more significantly, had been happily married to within a few weeks of his 60th anniversary.

'Losing JT is a devastating blow to Middlesex cricket,' John Emburey, the former off-spinner turned county president, said in the tribute I think Murray would have most appreciated. 'He was undoubtedly the finest wicketkeeper in the history of the club, and would be one of the first names on any team sheet when picking an all-time Middlesex XI. What he achieved is unlikely ever to be repeated. In many ways, it was fitting that his last day was spent at Lord's enjoying a home victory.'

I can only add that Murray was a cricketer and a man of the best kind, modest, brave, loyal and generous almost to a fault – and I might add palpably present while I've been remembering him, I hope to his honour, here.

# BIBLIOGRAPHY

Allen, D.R. (ed.), *Arlott on Cricket* (London: Collins, 1984)

Barrington, Ken, *Playing it Straight* (London: Stanley Paul, 1968)

Birley, Derek, *A Social History of English Cricket* (London: Aurum Press, 1999)

Close, Brian, *Close to Cricket* (London: Stanley Paul, 1968)

Cowdrey, Colin, *M.C.C.* (London: Hodder & Stoughton, 1976)

Dexter, Ted, *Ted Dexter Declares* (London, Stanley Paul, 1966)

Foot, David, *Beyond Bat and Ball* (London: Good Books, 1993)

Hill, Alan, *Bill Edrich: A Biography* (London: Andre Deutsch, 1994)

Howat, Gerald, *Len Hutton* (London: Heinemann, 1988)

Lemmon, David, *The History of Middlesex County Cricket Club* (London: A&C Black, 1988)

Peel, Mark, *Colin Milburn: Cricketing Falstaff* (London: Andre Deutsch, 1988)

Roberts, R.A., *The Fight for the Ashes 1961* (London: Harrap, 1961)

Snow, John, *Cricket Rebel* (London: Hamlyn, 1976)

Swanton, E.W., *Sort of a Cricket Person* (London: Collins, 1972)

Titmus, Fred, *Talk of the Double* (London: Stanley Paul, 1964)

*Wisden Cricketers' Almanack*, 1953–2019

# INDEX